ENDORSEMENTS

Wow, what a *tour de force*. In this book, Cheryl has shared a personal learning journey of how to create leadership through the application of six simple-to-follow, habits that make people feel good, create more independent and self-motivated teams, and deliver sustainable results. If you read just one book this year, make sure it is this one.

PROFESSOR PETER HINES
Enterprise Excellence Network

Let Go to Lead is for leaders who want to see their teams succeed independently. The book presents six habits and how to make them sustainable in a manner that is clear and concise, and most importantly, actionable. I have read many books on this topic and *Let Go to Lead* will add value to any leadership community.

BILLY RAY TAYLOR
Founder and CEO, LinkedXL and Author of *The Winning Link*

In *Let Go to Lead*, Cheryl Jekiel distills her decades of executive leadership insights, operational leadership experience, and consulting wisdom into an accessible and practical guide for embracing an open, values-centered, and humane approach to leadership. Her approach has proven to be not only effective but incredibly satisfying. This coaching style of leadership is rooted in her belief in the sacred value of humans, in sincere love for people, and in a desire to truly "champion their journeys." With warmth, humor, and candor, Cheryl guides leaders to create a trusting community where employees enjoy their work, contribute, improve, and stay to make a difference. She calls leaders to consistently practice leadership to be good at leadership and in these pages, Cheryl shows the way!

RENÉE SMITH
Founder and CEO of A Human Workplace

So many books on leadership tell you about great leaders, but they do not identify a roadmap a person can practice to become great. Cheryl has laid out six practical steps anyone can use to become more effective as a leader. Her writing derives from the results she has accomplished, and she is sharing her wisdom. I encourage readers to try the steps in the book - the world and our organizations need better leadership.

MICHAEL BREMER
Author of *How to Do a Gemba Walk*
Shingo Research & Professional Publication Award recipient

Cheryl Jekiel has an uncanny ability to insightfully capture lessons she has learned over a lifetime of being both a business practitioner and consultant and then turn those insights into easily learned and practiced habits. Her lessons come directly from her firsthand experiences, which she artfully describes in crisp examples and vignettes, and are thus readily recognizable and applicable to business life. Jekiel's six habits for effectively leading people remind me of the many lessons I learned while working for 20 years at a multi-national Japanese electronics manufacturer and the roles Japanese leaders play in leading their staff. By framing these habits in a Western context, her book will go a long way to bridging the gap between the mechanical "tools of Lean" and the true magic of a continuous improvement culture—people development.

PATRICK GRAUPP
Vice-President of TWI Institute
and author of *The TWI Workbook, Essential Skills for Supervisors*

In this world of ever-increasing people demands on business leaders, the people systems, and the habits we build into them are more critical than ever. There are so few leaders who have both the business experience AND the people system experience that Cheryl brings us in *Let Go to Lead*. So grateful for her willingness to share not only the why, but also the how to, with actionable and practical steps leaders can implement immediately.

MARC D BRAUN
Co-Founder | CEO | Coach - Encouraging Leaders

Let Go to Lead is a masterclass in empowering leaders to truly lead. The book is approachable, and the content is rich and actionable. It's full of great wisdom for leaders at every level. This is a proven process that Cheryl Jekiel is so generously sharing with all of us.

MARY PAT KNIGHT
Author of *The Humanized Leader*

As a leader, knowing how to intentionally create a culture of accountability can sometimes feel overwhelming and confusing. *Let Go to Lead* demystifies the process and provides six simple, but impactful habits to help any leader create a powerful organization.

JAY TIMMS MA, MS
Organizational Psychologist, Legendary Leaders

LET GO
TO LEAD

LET GO TO LEAD

Six Habits For Happier, More Independent Teams

(With Less Stress and More Time For Yourself)

CHERYL JEKIEL

Published and distributed by Merack Publishing
San Diego, USA
www.merackpublishing.com

Library of Congress Control Number: 2023918222

Jekiel, Cheryl
Illustrations created by Gerardo Romero Sainz. Mexico City, Mexico

*Let Go to Lead: Six Habits For Happier, More Independent Teams (With
Less Stress And More Time For Yourself)*

ISBNs
Paperback 978-1-957048-96-3
Hardcover 978-1-957048-98-7
eBook 978-1-957048-98-7

Ted, you are my best friend, and your
loving encouragement continues to cheer me on.

BEYOND A LEADERSHIP PROGRAM

Let Go to Lead is created based on the surprising lessons I learned while developing and expanding the CORE program over a number of years.

CORE combines a leadership development program with an implementation tool for any initiative or as a method to solve the people part of any problem. The work was designed for people-focused organizations that want to shift the styles of their leaders from chief problem solvers to a more empowering approach. In CORE, leaders learn to identify the specific behaviors they need from their teams to achieve the right results and use the **Performance Improvement Cycle** as a go-to model to master these skills.

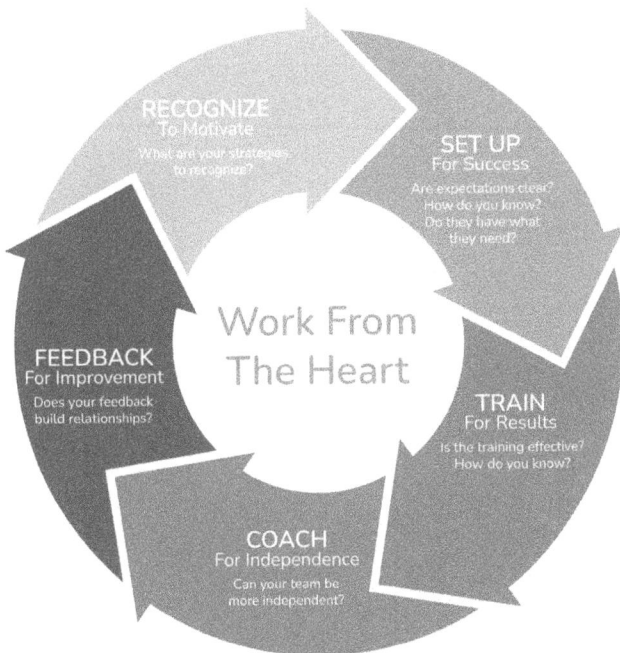

Performance Improvement Cycle

Each aspect of CORE is based upon a heart-based approach to cultivate relationships that support accountability and increase engagement. My original purpose was to assist organizations in developing leaders who could coach and develop their teams. What surprised me was that concepts from CORE helped organizations to successfully sustain behaviors for a broad range of initiatives – making it a priority to integrate CORE skills as required foundation for leadership. Over time, it became obvious that the elements of accountability in the Performance Improvement Cycle were also an innovative method to diagnose and solve the people part of any problem or challenge.

As an approach that *fundamentally changes workplace culture*, CORE provides all the tools needed to create a significant shift in a leadership community. The CORE program is designed to become a completely leader-led approach, since leaders learn what they teach (not what you tell them). In addition, leaders find the mostly interactive sessions a valuable opportunity to solve their own current business challenges with sufficient structure and support from others.

My intention with this book is to share what I witnessed in organizations that were finally able to achieve a coaching style of leadership that is well-suited for a workplace of highly engaged teams. In essence, the work of CORE has taught me what it takes for leaders to succeed, and in turn, I have described these lessons in *Let Go to Lead*.

CONTENTS

PART III

REBEL

Every day I work with frustrated leaders who have tried and failed to create independent team members. These dedicated leaders want to champion a workforce that lives to its full potential by developing their team's skills and talents, but nothing works well enough to sustain a successful, engaged workforce. Most of the time, I've witnessed leadership exhaust itself trying to make it happen, usually by conducting combinations of one-and-done training, external workshops, and other team-building activities.

Despite the time and resources spent, the reality of a happy, successful, independent workforce remains a distant dream. Frustrated, confused, and depleted from trying to do it all (including their team's jobs), leaders wonder what's gone wrong. Many of us have lived in the black-and-white world of exhaustion, never even dreaming that we could truly achieve the workplaces of our dreams, thinking it beyond our reach or capability. Most organizations I begin to work with haven't imagined, much less experienced, a highly engaged workforce. Instead their focus is on taking just the next step and being resolved to trying to make changes, rather than actually achieving success.

You can only create what you can imagine.

Your future vision, beyond your wildest dreams, isn't what I can imagine for your organization; it's what you will come to envision and create once you leverage the six habits in this book:

- Be Clear (Not Just In Your Own Head)
- Teach Them To Fish For Solutions (Don't Solve Their Problems)
- Take Responsibility (Stop Blaming)
- Let Go (Responsibly)
- Motivate More (Help Less)
- Level Your Team (Stop Training Them To Look Up)

When you practice them on the leadership journey, you will become the leader you've always wanted to be and enjoy life more. What would your life look like if you created an independent workforce? In this book, we will help you—the often overworked leader—avoid common stumbling blocks along the way. By cultivating the six habits in this book, you will be able to create an autonomous, accountable workforce through better relationships, and creating team members who are happier and more successful both inside and outside of the office.

But first, let's examine some common misconceptions about leaders. Why do workplaces have so few in leadership positions holding decision-making power over everyone else? In my experience, faulty thinking has led to the idea that leaders are inherently smarter or more capable of knowing what to do or how to solve problems. No one person holds a premium on good decisions.

During our work together, leaders have often commented that only people doing the work are experienced enough to make better decisions or solve the problems at hand. Leading from the top down in the traditional leadership model often creates team members who feel underestimated or underutilized. As a result, teams frequently aren't able to take full responsibility for their work and what they can accomplish. In fact, people can contribute *considerably more* than their roles ask of them.

> Why are team members underestimated or underutilized? There is a notable divide between our expectations and the actual range of talents and abilities of our workforce.

Once leaders break out of a traditional leadership style, they become more open to new opportunities. This enables them to reach goals they never have before—increasing their organization's ROI and transforming disengaged team members into people dedicated and invested in the organization's mission. I've seen these transformations for the past thirty years and wrote a book about continuous improvement and the role of human resources (where companies create a culture and align their workers to their mission). But my interest in the subject of work has had even deeper roots in my childhood.

I was not an easy child for my parents to guide through my early years. At seven years old, they put me in a combined classroom of first- and second-graders. Since there was no reason to wait, I completed all the first-grade books and then all the second-grade ones in a year. All go, go, go, I've never been a fan of the status quo. So, it's no surprise that at twelve years old, I had my first fairly decent job cleaning a large house after school.

Given my newfound joy of working, I really became interested in the topic of work and how to make it something better than what most people expect. That same year, I read the book *What Color Is Your Parachute?* and dreamed about becoming a career counselor someday in order to help others escape the fate of boring work or unfulfilling lives. Back then, I decided if I was going to spend my whole life working, I might as well love my job and do something worthwhile. Fast forward to when my parents told me it's only possible for me to go to a local college located in the middle of cornfields. My response? Working three jobs and saving enough money to attend the college of my dreams in downtown Chicago. Always the rebel.

In my twenties, I was fortunate to be a part of my first and most successful workplace transformation at a mid-size manufacturer of paper products called Sweetheart Cup. The company launched a complete shift in how people work as part of a larger corporate transformation. They enriched job descriptions to include problem-solving, teamwork, and handling their own product quality.

At the same time, they turned the role of leadership upside down in under a year and began re-qualifying supervisors for their jobs. Only candidates who were good at achieving success by inspiring their teams remained in supervisory positions. In other words, they kept leaders who could coach and not simply direct. As I witnessed the results, I became convinced that only historical practices kept the line between white-collar and blue-collar workers alive, creating a limiting power structure that wasn't optimal for anyone.

Many leaders in white-collar roles are comfortable, if not agreeable, with being in the driver's seat rather than handing the steering wheel to those they might believe are less capable. Even if team members in non-leadership roles, who are closer to the work and better informed, would make better decisions. By being stuck in the traditional leadership style, white-collar workers can hold back their companies from the many benefits of an independent workforce that leverages their teams' individual talents and abilities.

Sweetheart Cup cultivated a happy, independent workforce that created a sustainable change at the company. After witnessing the success of the turnaround, I dedicated my career to the development of workplaces that enrich people's work lives. In doing so, I discovered a simple truth—**when people are happy in their work, their lives undergo incredible improvements (like feeling energized from contributing more and the ability to live out their passions). Happiness at work brings increased harmony at home because people can spend more enjoyable time with loved ones.**

Along the way, I spent several years with a number of teams that implemented transformational leadership in many organizations, from various functional leadership roles. Human Resources was my favorite and closest to my calling. My passion for continuous improvement as the vehicle to unleash the passions of people in the workplace never ceased to drive my mission to positively impact how people work, and correspondingly how people lead. Eventually, I went out on my own to implement world-class HR systems in multiple workplaces. The experience sped up the pace of my knowledge in this area because I only focused on how to drive better results through engaged leadership that develops and inspires the talents of the workforce (some might call this having leaders get out of the way).

By this time, I became acutely aware that most organizations focused on continuous improvement struggled, if not failed, to generate sustainable improvements due to firmly entrenched traditional leadership styles. By traditional, I mean leaders who continually tell (advise) workers what to do and only sparingly involve employees in the solutions of how to direct or even improve the work. Then, sheer luck led me to help one of my earliest clients, a state agency, support their desire to drive a continuous improvement workplace. There, I witnessed my second successful leadership transformation.

When I built the new leadership program, it started off with the same simple idea which caused that first successful leadership transformation—make a typical leader more of a coach. Sounds good, right? But nobody seemed to know how to do it. It wasn't from a lack of trying, though. Most of the time, leaders applied the concept of coaching only when they needed to solve a problem. But I intuitively knew that people could never make coaching a habit if they didn't coach daily. Coaching needed to be integrated into the very definition of how people lead. It had to become a foundation of the basics of supervision.

In response, I assembled the continual lessons learned into a leadership program called "CORE" over the next several years. The name came from the idea that the skills and habits people would develop in the program would incorporate the basic definition of leadership. After its successful launch, its notable results surprised even me, but this was just the beginning. For example, one outstanding result occurred after leaders at the state agency created more independent team members. Reducing the supervisors' boring work made them feel good (and I'll talk more about that later). I also learned that great leadership feels good.

Over a number of years, I distilled the valuable cycles of lessons used in CORE into the six habits highlighted in this book, which have proven to be a recipe for how to lead effectively and have a more enjoyable life. I wanted to provide an impactful, successful way for every leader to approach their work. In these pages, I share the knowledge my team and I discovered while helping a number of organizations take their leadership to the next level for decades. Once you learn and practice these habits, you can use them to improve your own leadership and join with other leaders you know who want to do the same.

While incorporating the habits over time, we discovered leaders understand how to give up the short-term satisfaction of being in control and being "helpful," and instead trust their employees to do more of the heavy lifting. In doing so, leaders accomplished tasks that were more valuable and had more time to think strategically.

People don't change the way they do their jobs only for the company's benefit; they make changes because the experience feels good. And this has an incredible effect—**when people do something that feels good, it is also often good for the company**. In fact, the positive impact on the leaders' lives—not just the development of better skills—became one reason the pilot program expanded to include over three hundred and fifty leaders. They learned that when they led effectively, they had more time to enjoy life and do the things they love.

As time went on, even CORE's counterintuitive results surprised me. For instance, when leaders assumed the role of a coach rather than a director and shared their vulnerabilities and common challenges (instead of keeping them bottled up inside)—talking about how hard coaching is; how it's an uphill battle; difficulties with letting go of control; and wanting to end the trap of being a constant problem-solver—they made real progress in advancing their coaching skills right before my eyes.

> **What moves leadership from failed attempts at creating a coaching style of leadership to a successful transition? The human dynamic of a shared problem.**

There's something in their common struggle or problem that they can only tackle together, never apart. I watched this positive transformation happen daily. When people identify this shared cause, they cease to be driven by their own (sometimes competing) interests and coalesce as a team. Previously, my experience showed that people rarely talked about their struggles at work. But during CORE, when leaders shared their worries and challenges, they grew exponentially as leaders.

I didn't know that when we developed CORE as a community of practice, it would be a slam-dunk productivity, revenue, and goal enhancer. Or that its range of benefits would include more enjoyment of life and leadership. Creating optimal engagement begins with six habits that disrupt the traditional leadership dynamic and create ways for you to coach your team members to become more independent. Once developed, you will break free of what I refer to as "**stuckness**"— getting so lost in "doing" that you don't take the time to reflect on the best ways to get work done and support your team. The first step in getting results beyond your wildest dreams is learning how to get "unstuck."

STUCKNESS

Over the years, I encountered many organizations trying to shift their leaders from a directorial, tell-them-what-to-do style into a coaching kind of leadership. I remember hosting an event where I asked the leadership of a large group of companies if they had made satisfactory progress in a number of improvement strategies, and many raised their hands for different options. Then I asked if they were satisfied with how they were developing their leaders' ability to coach continuous improvement efforts. Not one person raised their hand (forget about entire companies). Mic drop. Instead, they shared their struggles about finding any effective approach to help their leaders develop a continually improving, highly engaged workforce.

No matter what anyone tried, nothing worked on a large scale. And yet, I had observed that some leaders were natural coaches, inclined to develop their team members to be more independent. However, many leaders appear to be mired in directorial approaches, which kept them in unsuccessful cycles of team development. I discovered that the adage *if only I knew better* doesn't really hold true when it comes to the training and development of leaders. It's not enough to know what to do, but to actually **do** it. In this book, you will learn the six habits that will help you become the leader you always wanted to be (Part I) and also learn how to practice them so you can lead more successful teams and find more time to enjoy life (Part II).

This chapter highlights how leaders get stuck on the road to developing their coaching skills. You might see yourself in many of the examples; but don't worry, you can be free of the common missteps I've discovered. The six leadership habits in this book will help you avoid these sticking points. You will become clear about defining success to get the results you want from your team, build your ability to develop them, and learn how to nurture everyone's abilities to unleash their talents.

As you become "unstuck," you will learn how to best guide your team, to accomplish what's needed, and to ensure that you don't backslide into your old "doing" and "directing" comfort zone. You will finally get comfortable by being less controlling and giving less advice as you become more of a coach. When you connect with other leaders, you will feel less alone and have opportunities to make new friendships. As you practice your coaching style of leadership, you will begin to see the value of recognizing productive behaviors without threatening consequences, leading to a positive work environment that feels good. Now, let's reflect on where leaders get stuck.

PEOPLE AREN'T MIND READERS

Over the last several years, nine out of ten leaders I've worked with have stated that unclear expectations are the reason teams don't perform the way they need to. This discovery is even more profound because leaders have little to no awareness that their failure to communicate clear expectations is why they don't have the results they want or where they get stuck. This common blind spot shocks many leaders. It's an incredible place to get stuck because setting clear expectations is the starting line in the process of leadership. The beauty of fixing this problem is simple and challenging at the same time. Being clear requires reflection, collaboration, clear communication, and confirming what people understand. I will talk much more about this in the first habit— Be Clear (Not Just In Your Own Head).

WORKING HARD IS NOT ALWAYS SMART

Stuckness happens when our constant multitasking causes us to lose sight of the specific things we need to do to move our team forward. We can get so lost in "doing" that we don't take the time to reflect on the best ways to get our work done and support our team. Teams can be challenging to manage because leaders aren't sure what's not working. And that lack of clarity can lead to blaming, which is talked about in more detail in the third habit, Take Responsibility (Stop Blaming).

Being overwhelmed with "doing" stands in the way of real progress. I talk more about how to break this cycle in the second and fourth habit, Teach Them To Fish For Solutions (Don't Solve Their Problems) and Let Go (Responsibly). Somehow, it seems leaders believe that by just working hard—really hard—they will get everything done. It can feel almost impossible to do things a new way, even when you know that you'd do well to develop your team and be more of a coach. The *Harvard Business Review* had some interesting advice about solving this common problem.

"Consider professional soccer goalies and their strategies for defending against penalty kicks. According to a study by Michael Bar-Eli and colleagues, those who stay in the center of the goal, rather than leaping to the right or left, perform the best: They have a 33.3% chance of stopping the ball. Nonetheless, goalies stay in the center only 6.3% of the time. Why? Because it looks and feels better to have missed the ball by diving, even if it turns out to have been in the wrong direction, than to have stood still and watched the ball sail by.

The same aversion to inaction holds true in the business world. When we surveyed participants in our executive education classes, we found that managers feel more productive executing tasks than planning them. Especially when under time pressure, they perceive planning to be wasted effort."

"WHY ORGANIZATIONS DON'T LEARN,"
HARVARD BUSINESS REVIEW

The article lists **exhaustion** and **lack of reflection** as the two challenges to this kind of busyness, saying, **"Being 'always on' doesn't give leaders time to reflect on what they did well and what they did wrong."** The article also referred to actual research about the difference between reflection and non-reflection, where some workers had been given time to reflect during the start of their initial training. The ones who had reflection time performed more than twenty percent better on average than those who didn't. They did similar studies on college students and employees in a variety of organizations that produced the same results.

Just the other day, I was talking to a plant manager, who went on about his busy schedule and frustration over daily back-to-back meetings. I found myself thinking that he would be so much better off if he took a half hour a day to just stop and think things through. Taking time to think and reflect breaks the cycle of "doing." Scheduling time for reflection into your team's schedules also promotes their relaxation and rejuvenation to help beat exhaustion.

LEADERS ARE NOT CHIEF PROBLEM-SOLVERS

Many leaders feel that part of working hard involves funneling every problem their way. After all, they believe management selected them for leadership because of their capability. So in their mind, leadership means taking on the role of chief problem-solver. Yet, this belief system not only puts limitations on team members but also is an exceedingly stressful way for a leader to live. To handle every problem, these leaders often work late hours and on weekends. When they aren't at the office, work preoccupies them much of the time. Sound familiar?

Are you exhausted from carrying around everyone's problems and the responsibility for their solutions?

A lot of behaviors contribute to "stuckness," including leaders with good intentions who sometimes encounter big learning curves while developing their coaching skills. Most leaders don't recognize they're "stuck" in traditional leadership roles, frequently overlooking the need to exercise all the elements of accountability for their teams and instead focus on their role of providing all the answers. But once leaders try new ways of implementing accountability, they see that they and their teams can live to their fullest potential by simply allowing workers to solve their own problems.

Many leaders don't know how they're getting in their own way.

In the supervisor example earlier, when I developed CORE within a state agency, the "stuckness" problem and its solution were surprising. Normally, leadership has such a difficult time changing their habits, training is usually ineffective. The real shift came from their shared experience. **The supervisors began to discuss what they were there to do and analyzed why they had a line of people standing outside of their cubes—what was it that people didn't know or didn't know how to do that caused them to stand in line to get the answer?** As the leaders compared experiences, they discovered how they could coach their team members to be more independent.

After implementing the changes, the supervisors watched and felt the shift—no more lines. **When they shifted, they were happier.** And that's when I first saw, in a very visual way, the power of coaching team members toward this new independence. I had never seen leaders actually change until that time at the state agency, where they became coaches, changing their behavior and experiencing the win of that shift.

Relapsing into Old Mindsets

When I returned six months later, I got an even bigger surprise. A lot of the supervisors had gone back to their old ways. Some parts of their new leadership skills weren't holding. Mindset issues came back into the picture, making them think that people on their team weren't ready to be accountable to solve their own problems or didn't have the proper focus to solve them for a variety of reasons. Other leaders had reverted to reacting negatively in situations instead of making choices about how to respond effectively.

They'd gotten stuck again.

But I shouldn't have been surprised. The supervisors' new behaviors weren't strong enough yet to utilize the training to create a different long-term experience. The way people handle stress can cause them to revert to old mindsets and/or behaviors and slip into traditional leadership roles that tend to promote a lack of accountability. Expecting the change to be sustainable after a two-session training would be like expecting people with any type of ingrained habits to build new behaviors in a two-weekend workshop.

We also found most, if not all, leaders were a long way from making the concepts of effective leadership their "go-to" style. They had been absorbing the new ideas to 'take them for a whirl' in the practice time provided in the program, but found themselves stuck because they didn't know how and when to apply the new approaches they had learned.

IT'S HARD TO CHANGE HABITS, REALLY HARD

Does your leadership get stuck in old patterns? We've all been there. Training doesn't build habits. So, what's the solution? I happened across how to overcome this kind of "stuckness" by accident at the state agency when the supervisors' lines went down and they became happier. Like many organizations, they hadn't made the connection between entry-level supervisory training and how to teach coaching skills to obtain the benefits of adopting excellent HR practices. At its best, participants would say things like—*I'm glad I came, Now I know what I don't know*— but they didn't create any real change.

When asked to provide feedback on their program, given my world-class HR expertise, the agency gave me the opportunity to develop the training, and a powerful shift occurred. The success of that program, where we had notable success in building a coaching style of leadership, changed the focus of my work for the rest of my professional life.

Team members changed their behavior, which led to the kind of success they didn't believe was possible and gave them the confidence that came with it. The overall approach to leadership transformed from a traditional one that got "stuck" in telling people what to do (creating long lines outside their cubicles) to one that increasingly unleashed the talents of team members (no lines). However, my revision of the training wasn't the key driver of the success. The largely unexpected lessons I've learned along the way continued to teach me how leaders can get themselves unstuck, which had nothing to do with any "miraculous" training class. I go into more detail about how to keep a highly engaged workforce in the fifth habit, Motivate More (Help Less).

After witnessing how simply training people to be better leaders didn't work, I leveraged my basic supervisory instruction experiences from my early years as head of HR. **While developing the introductory leadership training, I restructured all the concepts of a leadership development program to make it simple, memorable, relatable, and lasting.** For example, organizations usually created training from a white-collar management perspective, so the viewpoint didn't resonate with everyone. In addition, much of the available training was big on using lingo that you need to be "in the club" to understand. In response, I developed the training with common terms and clear language everyone understood.

Prior programs also didn't tie training concepts together, so I developed a memorable model that established the go-to behaviors that would constantly guide leaders years after learning them. In addition, we designed the leadership program to be more experiential so people could **practice** the behaviors and learn what to **do** and not just raise their awareness, which was one of the biggest takeaways of the program.

Experts in how people learn also gave some good input into the new program, focusing on how to create the most effective approaches for people to learn. I built upon their recommendations by emphasizing the need for team members and leaders to **reflect** and make better plans. This led to the development of a less transactional and more transformative approach to leadership training, creating leaders who would coach their team members to be more independent. The program participants had two days of training, one month off, and then two more days of training.

LEADERS CAN KEEP STRUGGLES PRIVATE

In the process of doing the exercises, leaders shared their experiences and became more vulnerable with each other. Over and over again, I found that a key to the success of the program comes from creating a leadership community experience that produces a change in behavior. Aha! People sharing their problems (or their stuckness) boosted their confidence to keep trying. While not a particularly new lesson, it hadn't occurred to me just how important this would be in the future of sustainable leadership training. **The good news is that creating a leadership community is not something that requires training or special resources. It's available to every organization that chooses to spend the time and resources to make it happen.**

STUCK ON THE STICKS

One topic that continued to show up had to do with leaders who seemed reluctant, if not resentful, about positively motivating their teams, saying, "Why should I say 'good work' for simply doing their job?"

They often shared that their supervisors didn't recognize them very much for a job well done and remained convinced they shouldn't need to treat their teams any differently. "After all, I turned out okay," they would say. However, this trend revealed how threatening environments shaped leaders—a sort of *do it, or else or deal with the consequences* philosophy. The idea of positively motivating people didn't register. It's hard to have a habit that you've never seen before. As a leader, you can't discipline your way into the greatest levels of engagement. I talk more about this in the sixth habit, Level Your Team (Stop Training Them To Look Up).

Answering Every Question

Picture a big room in a large public office space. Six supervisors sat in the room in high-top cubicles. Most people read their leadership styles by the size of the line outside their cube. One might assume a long line as a sign of the supervisor's expertise, thinking people lined up to talk to the best supervisor because of their valued opinion. Conversely, people might think that the ones with short or no lines were not that good at their jobs. At the end of the second round of training, the supervisors made some real shifts in behavior, interesting changes I hadn't expected.

One told me, "If someone comes in and asks how they're supposed to fill out their claim, I ask them where they could go to look up the answer."

Another said, "I ask them to look up the answer, and then come back with questions if they have them."

The lines outside of the cubicles began to vanish.

As the supervisors worked on the concepts for becoming more of a coach, the team changed their behavior. They no longer felt responsible to answer their team's questions. Instead, they encouraged those who needed help to be more independent. It was a fundamental change in taking responsibility and being accountable. When supervisors turned their focus away from answering questions, the lines stopped. They let go of the illusion that if they kept answering questions, fewer mistakes would be made, contributing to smoother results that they could control.

After spending time practicing together, the supervisors started saying things like—*I'm liking my life better, I'm leaving work on time, I hadn't realized that I had been carrying these problems on my back.* Essentially, when the supervisors struggled to drive real accountability by constantly answering every question, they had absorbed everything that wasn't working in the department and carried all that home with them. They also realized they didn't have time to improve the process of adjudication, create better training, or improve their service because people kept lining up outside their cubicles wanting answers they could find for themselves.

GETTING "UNSTUCK"

In order to assume new roles and change lifestyles, team members have to do more to change their mindsets and behaviors. To meet this need, we expanded CORE's community of practice from one month to one year, which was a big step toward ensuring organizations stay unstuck. The added time enabled them to create lasting changes over a longer period with incredible results—truly engaging team members with limitless potential to unleash their talents. Even after the one-year program, groups have a range of approaches to maintain their ongoing leadership skill practice. One of the most effective long-term ways to support the new behaviors is to have the existing, higher-level leaders teach the elements of accountability and coaching to newer participants.

PEOPLE MUST LIKE AND ENJOY THE WORK THEY DO

We concentrate on what makes leaders feel good because it's human nature to repeat activities that have a positive effect. If a leader has a new leadership style, they need to create self-reinforcing behavior to keep it up. People will resist any change that doesn't actually feel better in the end.

Every people-metric improves when leaders have better relationships with their teams. When we coach team members to be more independent, we see increases in engagement. As engagement increases attendance improves, tardiness lessens, safety also improves, there's better retention, and better attraction of quality employees. We know that positive, empowering leadership creates a better workforce and improves all the metrics, particularly financial results. Generally, as stated in *Employee Engagement: Tools for Analysis, Practice, and Competitive Advantage*, it's worth seven to eleven percent of profitability to have improved engagement, which is more valuable than most cost-saving initiatives. The community of leaders within an organization can only achieve this impressive ROI together.

CORE simply teaches the basics of how to show up as a leader when working with people. Others describe the program as the fundamentals of accountability. It's not a pill or a fix, and it's certainly not the only way to get unstuck. However, we hope this book gives you some ideas about what you can do to improve your leadership or organization.

BEYOND STUCKNESS

Are you a leader who already knows you need to get "unstuck" and are being asked to figure it out? Have you been so overloaded and overwhelmed you didn't even know you were stuck? Too busy taking on your team's problems, working too many hours, and being told you need to be more of a coach but don't know how?

If you have no idea what lies beyond these problems, you have lots of company. The vast majority of organizations, and the leaders within them, have no experience beyond these types of "stuckness." In the next chapter, we'll invite you to consider what your life would look like when your teams are much more independent, creating a level of engagement you hadn't dared envision before.

A FUTURE VISION FOR A HIGHLY ENGAGED CULTURE
(ENVISION YOUR EMERALD CITY)

The story of the "Land of Oz" has come up a number of times during my life to show me how to learn about what is possible beyond what I could only see—like when the wizard pulls the levers that control the "great and powerful Oz" from behind a curtain. I have a gigantic poster of *The Wizard of Oz* in my house. For those unfamiliar with the 1939 movie starring Judy Garland, it's a story about a girl named Dorothy and was the first film to use Technicolor film. Prior to that, every movie on screen was only filmed in black and white.

Why do I have a poster of the movie on my wall at home? When I dated my husband of thirty-plus years, we decided to take a break. I needed more time to figure out whether I wanted to be in a serious relationship. He agreed, but suggested we honor this decision with a nice dinner, and we watched *The Wizard of Oz*. It was a meaningful way to celebrate our friendship, which might or might not have stood the test of time. The tender way he took the pressure off of me and the message of the movie, *there's no place like home*, still makes me smile. Little did we know that it would work out and we would live a life beyond our wildest dreams. I equate the Land of Oz or the Emerald City to be the promise of a brilliant future.

The first time I saw a truly highly engaged workforce, I said, "This is like the Land of Oz!" It was my only way to describe what I had not seen yet and was beyond my wildest dreams. The magic of the Emerald City isn't found in the clicking of Dorothy's ruby slippers (which she discovers will carry her back home if she taps them three times), but rather the awareness that she gained when she realized she already had what she needed to get her where she most wanted to go.

And so do you.

You may not be able to see your "Emerald City" yet, but it's a place where you've achieved truly sustainable, desired results. Where you get your life back, free from carrying the weight of the world on your shoulders, by holding people accountable and allowing them to unleash their talents, which makes them happier and more engaged. Oz is where you drive your organization to exponential success by creating caring, supportive relationships and an engaged workplace where people want to work.

After Dorothy's house spins wildly in the twister that lands her over the rainbow, she journeys to the Emerald City—the capital of a world beyond her dreams. I'll never forget the beginning of *The Wizard of Oz*, when Dorothy steps out of her black-and-white world filled with problems and struggles and into Technicolor Oz. Just imagine what you might see when you succeed in having an accountable, autonomous, highly engaged workforce. You will step out of your typical world of work, filled with trials and tribulations, into a brand-new world where teamwork and positivity create miracles you never dreamed of, even spilling over into your personal life.

How is that possible?

THE MOMENTUM OF AN ENGAGED WORKFORCE

Think about that twister for a minute. When negative things spiral out of control, morale problems occur; poor morale makes people really unhappy; unhappy people make other people unhappy, and productivity gets worse. However, the same effect holds true for happiness and positive morale. The more people identify and resolve problems, the happier people get; the happier people get, the more they're engaged; the more they're engaged, the more leaders find it easier to be positive and open to changes. Positivity and openness to change bring more confidence and happiness to the team, which creates even better results. Everything gets better.

The morale of an organization feeds off of itself in either a positive or negative direction. I usually point out that if people are missing the positive in their organization, they are likely sitting in the negative spiral. In my experience, morale or the level of engagement isn't stationary or static.

Consider whether your workforce is spiraling in an upward or a downward motion. Are there significant issues such as poor leadership that seem to be bringing people down or making them less invested in success? Or, do you see influences that drive higher morale, such as people feeling more connected to the greater mission of your organization because they have the tools they need to improve their situations?

One of the hallmarks of having a clear vision of your "Emerald City" is how positive morale develops a momentum all its own. Many organizations even bring customers to their workplace to reveal the competitive edge of a workforce that is deeply involved in their work and customer-focused. When leaders coach their staff, over time they create such a workforce, which opens teams and their organizations up to many other positive results.

When clients become diligent in their pursuit of empowering leadership, I'm frequently asked to describe how their lives will be different once they've powered through their long-standing struggles and created a problem-solving workforce—*What does it look like when we get there? What would happen to the way we do our work? And how would it be different?*

Most of the teams I work with are fairly knowledgeable about how to work together to identify issues, resolve them, and come up with better ideas about what to do to make them happen. But when an organization really begins to enter their own Emerald City, somewhere they've never experienced before, teams are free to implement their own ideas.

One example of still being on the journey to somewhere brand new happens when teams give leadership their ideas and then only leadership gets to decide anything, buy anything, judge an idea as good or bad, or when and how to act upon it. When those decisions are all management-led, organizations will have workforces that will struggle with engagement. Instead, by allowing teams to identify and solve issues, help fix things, order supplies, build things, and change processes, teams get to use their skills and talents and engage on a deep level.

HOW MUCH ENGAGEMENT DO YOU REALLY WANT?

The idea of teams that don't need supervision unsettles most organizations. But if management continues to make all the decisions about implementation, organizations won't improve much, and their workforces disengage. Sometimes leaders respond to the idea of engaged teams by saying—*Oh, we already tried that, I don't need to try that again,* or *They don't know how to do it*—killing ideas fast.

In a number of training sessions over the years, I've asked employees and leaders if they ever gave someone a suggestion for improvement and it didn't go well. For example, their idea got shut down, someone didn't get back to them, or they received some other negative response. Then I asked those who answered "yes" if they gave that person another idea afterward. The response is always the same—never. One rejection and they're done.

Getting to where you really want to go requires leaders to nurture open communication that is safe from recrimination or retribution. It is a place where teams constantly share their ideas, fix problems, and improve the organization.

When leaders first begin the program, many department heads tell me their team doesn't have any ideas. Thirty people in their department without any ideas? Hard to believe, right? But, if that really is true, then odds are the team has learned that the department head doesn't want to know about their ideas. But most leaders don't even know how to handle them. Most of them aren't able to assimilate their team's thinking. Even if they do try the suggestion and it doesn't work, they don't know how to give constructive criticism.

When leaders protect their teams' ideas, they will keep sharing.

If leaders aren't careful, they can cause a lot of damage. When a team member goes up to bat for the first time to share an idea and it gets shot down immediately, it's almost worse than if the team member never tried sharing their idea. An employee thought their leader cared and valued their opinion. All it takes is a busy leader who reacts in a reflex response like *we already tried that* to kill an idea and close down communication. Those leaders didn't mean to kill the idea, but they did. Then trust breaks down with their team.

Leaders show respect for their team by incorporating their ideas. They ask for opinions, suggestions, and encouragement. Leaders make it clear that they believe in their teams' talents and want to develop them.

And when those talents flourish, leaders are there to protect them. I worked in an environment that had the most highly engaged team I'd ever seen. Team members fought over finding solutions to problems. They were clearly happy in the absence of control, and the experience forever changed me. When something went wrong, they'd be on top of each other trying to get to a resolution. While I was there, the team let me know they needed help to figure out a process for when something goes wrong. They wanted to know how to approach solving the problem in an organized manner, so they literally didn't run into each other.

The leaders there all spoke often about feeling out of control. They would say the solutions were great in the end, but they just had to realize that their teams were going to solve the problem in ways that they wouldn't.

Leaders have to be aware that the flow of the work isn't driven by them. It is about being in the flow, and people in the process drive it.

Imagine creating a workplace where people doing the work are actually happy. One guy told me the other day, "When we have problems, we sit down at the table and just work our shit out. That's what we do. We just work our stuff out."

I've been quoting him since that day because this relatively young man understood that when you're on a successful team, you have to work together closely and need to resolve issues that arise. They don't ignore things, bury them, or waste energy giving each other a hard time. Instead, they talk over their differences or hurt feelings to get on the same page. In some environments, instead of taking steps to take care of a problem, they want to be "nice" and just refuse to address situations.

Other employees default to a mindset of doing *whatever my boss thinks*. Later in the book, I discuss the important habit of training your people to not look up. The team in this workplace was one of the first I had met that didn't look up. They only focused on each other and the results they achieved as a group. They decided what they thought was the right thing to do on merit, not based on what those above wanted or thought.

But in this example, team members didn't care about any of that pretense. They've realized how much energy gets eaten up out of so-called "respect" of the higher-ups. It's why I remind people in my program that if you think they pay your paycheck, they don't. The customers do. You work for the customers. There's a lot of reverence for people in power who can lead to employees who are busy making sure what they're doing is "right" rather than pleasing the customer, like getting something to them on time.

A WORKPLACE CAPABLE OF R-E-S-P-E-C-T

Aretha Franklin's attention-getting song brings to mind what I've witnessed in the work of CORE, really meeting the needs of the leaders. I've found that the word "respect" is thrown around in continuous improvement work environments all the time. It's an easy word to throw around; however, I don't just want to talk about respect, but rather create a place that could actually promote and foster that genuine behavior among leaders and their teams. I wanted to get above the banter and create respectful environments. Through the work we have done in CORE, we've discovered that the most respectful thing we can do for leaders is to give them what they need for their jobs.

Imagine a workplace where leaders and teams respect each other. A world where you work your stuff out by inviting each other to sit down at the table. But, those interpersonal relationships are not easy. Since people don't come out of high school or college knowing these skills, CORE develops interpersonal skills through various concepts. One of my larger clients uses a few dozen of them to help employees grow their skills with messages like—*be curious, don't polarize, don't take positions.* These reminders help people communicate in ways that keep them from being at odds with each other by focusing on and reinforcing simple skills.

What would it look like to have a workplace where leaders make expectations clear to set their teams up for success? Address conflicts in constructive ways so the team's energy is spent on the job at hand? Make resources available to their team so they feel empowered to make decisions and solve their problems?

When leaders stop trying to get out in front of their team, they can concentrate on having a more effective, supporting role and lead from behind. During one of my workshops, I spotted this concept for the first time with my own eyes. We would tear the room apart—turn the tables and the speaker's podium upside down, and put chairs at odd angles everywhere. When the attendees came back from lunch, we asked them to put the room back together to make it the most effective for our work that afternoon. Thirty people started processing the scene, the request, and what they were going to do. Usually, a leader will step up and start to direct traffic. And that's what happened that afternoon.

Someone eventually said something like, "We're going to do it like this."

But then the real leader walked up to the "take-charge" person and suggested in a whisper, "If you have those people do this, that may work better."

Great leadership isn't about being the one giving commands. It's not about fighting for leadership.

Imagine leaders supporting a team member's problem-solving. They suggest and work in sync with another's vision, helping that person become more successful in what they're doing. By just contributing some thoughts and ideas in a supportive way, a person can consider and choose how to act. Ever since then, I believe "helping" is the model for every great leader.

Most days, I help leaders who are leading a team that has a leader. They are a level above the leader. I usually warn them to be careful and caution them from trying to overtake their teams directly. It's not only disrespectful, but that interference makes the actual leader feel less like the leader. Great leaders make sure their actions support people in their vision instead of somehow overtaking them.

If you were to achieve your vision for engagement, consider how leaders walk softly and more carefully—*What will I say? When will I say it? How will I say what I'm going to say?* The story about the real leader whispering in the ear of the person who took charge in the example above shows us what that process looks like. It's so subtle most people won't notice. The team might not be aware of it, but the helping hand is there, leaving everything else untouched. Leaders say things like—*I'm here to help you, I'm here to support you, I'm here to lift you up, I'm here to make sure you feel better than you normally do, I want you to feel like you can do things you didn't think you could do before.*

YOUR YELLOW BRICK ROAD TO SUCCESS

For the last several years, I've been teaching the six habits in this book to teams who have used them to get unstuck and expand their companies in new, exponential ways. Creating more independent team members unleashes the power of decision-making and problem-solving skills inherent in everyone. When people incorporate the habits, they become more responsible, accountable, and autonomous by engaging in their own problem-solving. This creates greater opportunities to be more fully who they are—understanding themselves better and growing in profound ways, personally and professionally.

The leadership habits I'll explore in this book will help you discover your unique yellow brick road to success. You will find your best version of the "Emerald City" when people follow it to unleash their talents, not just the chosen few. Through the six simple habits that follow, you'll create joyful workplaces where your leadership targets become a reality. Using CORE's Performance Improvement Cycle—featuring the key leadership principles we promote—not only makes leaders more effective but also builds relationships that increase accountability and autonomy. The road to building the leadership abilities of your dreams begins with clarity, the number one habit you will need to lead successfully so you can get your life back.

GETTING MORE OUT OF LIFE

As I've said before, this journey is hard. So why go through all the hassle? How can asking a bunch of open-ended questions turn into anything?

I encourage leaders to hang on through the hard part, because soon, when you arrive at your "Emerald City," you'll wonder why you were ever doubtful. **Quality of life increases when there is less work to do, and strategic impact also increases because you will finally have time to contribute more.** Not only are there new opportunities for growth at work, but you will have time left over to enjoy your personal life. Let's visualize what getting your life back looks like.

In the beginning of our program, leaders had lost the ability to get out from under their day-to-day struggles, so there were more fires to put out than necessary each week, which resulted in serious burnout. They could avoid this needless energy drain with strategic thinking. Leaders have a hard time seeing the 60,000-foot view of their team's mission if they're stuck in the weeds solving problems that are best left to their team. And the effects can be devastating.

Instead, you can live the life of the leader you always wanted to be. Just imagine—

- Spending an entire afternoon thinking about and putting into place your long-term plan?
- Leaving the office at a reasonable time, attending kids' athletic events, and still having time to eat dinner with the family?
- Giving up crisis management for a peace plan—a long-term strategy to build effectiveness and drive better results every day?
- All the monkeys on your back disappear.

When you no longer take on the weight of what you see as the burdens of your position, great things happen for everybody. You will be better able to influence others positively because you simply have more energy. When team members contribute more, the process buys you more time and delivers much better solutions. With ownership interest, team members become true partners ready to take part in problem-solving. And when that happens, you are free to think bigger and get out of the way of the team members who have learned how to handle issues themselves.

Once the team coalesces, there is more of an ability to trust in the process of their independence. And you will enjoy the powerful feeling of hanging back and letting your team speak for the department or company. The team receives a lift, which makes them more effective, owning their responsibility to come up with successful solutions and reaping the rewards of their ownership.

One woman in the state agency example in the "Stuckness" chapter commented powerfully after her team had found their solutions. When the lines went down at the cubicles, the supervisor said, **"I never realized how much I carried around. As I leave work at five, I'm done. I'm out. I never had that before."**

By breaking the patterns of control and the definition of work in that department, she allowed her team to explore their own paths. Members solved their own problems—maybe not perfectly, but that journey empowered them beyond measure. The results achieved by her team enabled the supervisor to get her own job done, which she hadn't had time to do, maybe ever.

Coaching team members to be more independent has bumps in the road, but it will always be more powerful than traditional hierarchical leadership. **When you arrive at the place where your team members solve their own problems, you will see how far you and your team have come and never want to go back to the old ways.**

In one way, coaching team members is the steepest climb we can make as a leader. It's much harder than we pretend. But becoming aware and leaning into the difficulty of this evolution makes the journey easier. For example, you don't want to climb a mountain if you're only prepared for a stroll. **We need to be clear that this leadership style of coaching is a straight-up climb.** And how do climbers survive unforeseen challenges? Preparation. When we are clear about how hard the evolution can be, then we can stay grounded in the concepts when the journey gets rough.

Be Advised That This Is a Journey Few Have Made Before

Most people intent on reaching the goal of continuous improvement have stayed stuck. Interventions like workshops and trainings in the past weren't long enough to take hold so that leaders could practice their new coaching skills sufficiently. When pressures rise, supervisors often default to what they know and leave their coaching skills behind. This usually gets them into worse trouble because team members continue to waste their time instead of solving their problems.

To avoid these pitfalls and better prepare for the journey, let's get a better sense of the rocky path to this kind of leadership style. In the beginning, the biggest obstacle to leaders growing into coaches is failing to understand that the shift is a sea change in the way they run their day-to-day. A change so big, some days it can feel like they are steering an aircraft carrier with a paddle. A company learns about the idea of coaching and wants to implement it in their organization. They develop a program as a resource for employees to learn some necessary skills.

Everybody knows what good training is. But often it isn't effective in this coaching style of leadership. People want the change, but they aren't ready or willing to do the work it takes to get those results, no matter how beneficial. **Implementing short-term coaching training is like**

climbing Everest but forgetting to bring a jacket. Call it denial or just poor planning, but most companies rely on short-term training to create transformations among their leaders.

Growing into successful, groundbreaking leadership—like the community created when leaders coach team members to be independent—takes time and dedication to nurture and develop. When leaders have arrived and seen the benefits of this leadership style—empowering teams more fully, expanding their teams' skills or abilities, taking time off while resting easy (because the teams know what to do)—they are better able to make the kinds of personal changes necessary for the new behavior of coaching, instead of constantly directing.

The skills that come with this evolution teach us when to direct, train, mentor, and coach. Sometimes coaching is just encouragement, instilling a belief in the hearts of team members that they can solve whatever problem comes their way. When team members and supervisors work like this in community, unleashing everyone's potential, the company finally harnesses the powerful ability to meet and exceed goals. The focus is no longer on one-and-done trainings, where leaders fall into a constant state of direction.

Old Ways Can Die Hard

But even with the best of intentions and applications, the journey to this kind of freedom and stellar results can stall out somewhere along the way if leaders can't release control. They don't even recognize when it's happening. On their own, they are doing the best they can. But when certain cues trigger old personal habits, leaders fall into their old, traditional leadership style, and coaching gives way to constant direction. The old dynamic of problem-solving and, in turn, receiving gratitude takes over the newer good feeling that comes from helping others develop their own abilities.

But there are many other reasons for this kind of stall, including the pressures of leadership. Team members working at cross purposes, someone banging on their door, staffing shortages worsening, and a whole range of other problems could cause leaders to revert to old, more comfortable habits and ways of thinking. During times of stress, it's just more familiar to direct and seek gratification the old way, instead of exercising their new coaching muscle. Also, an unpleasant coaching experience—like delegating work when someone isn't ready that results in a major mistake—may cause the supervisor to mistakenly believe that giving up control is never good. Lastly, fear sometimes sets in as we discussed earlier, like—*the team will screw things up* or *my way is the only way*. Leaders can't coach team members if they're constantly on their heels.

Lots of times, human resource departments don't have a leadership program robust enough to keep leaders on track for this kind of evolution. We can make a case that no one does leadership development very well, and only have to look at the "Great Resignation" to understand the need for a sea change in leadership. Why millennials leave the workforce is key to understanding the phenomenon, which includes the lack of fulfillment they feel in their current roles. Like millions of Americans, they want to find a new way to work. Tired of the stress and burnout, many have walked out on their jobs and others have plans to do so, according to the Deloitte Global 2022 Gen Z and Millennial Survey:

"Meanwhile, burnout is very high among both generations, and signals a major retention issue for employers:

- 46% of Gen Zs and 45% of millennials feel burned out due to the intensity/demands of their working environments.

- 44% of Gen Zs and 43% of millennials say many people have recently left their organization due to workload pressure.

Employers do seem to be making progress when it comes to prioritizing mental health and well-being in the workplace. More than half agree that workplace well-being and mental health has become more of a focus for their employers since the start of the pandemic. However, there are mixed reviews on whether the increased focus is actually having a positive impact."

According to the survey, the need for support in their roles is key among the group. This also points out the strength of their need to balance the challenges of their everyday lives with advocating for societal change. HR departments haven't pivoted to meet this challenge and sometimes even get in the way.

But when the journey comes to an end, and leaders have met the moment and coached team members after realizing all its benefits, there are still things that can derail the hard work that has taken place. A switch of some kind, such as a change in the organization, can sideswipe these good practices for some time. Occasionally, a culture of command and control can take over and test leadership.

However, once people have lived the dream, it's hard to go back. A happy ending comes when supervisors internalize the coaching leadership style. Once accomplished, it's difficult to shake loose.

PART I

SIX HABITS THAT WILL TURN YOU INTO THE LEADER YOU ALWAYS WANTED TO BE

By now you're wondering, how do I get unstuck? You might also wonder if it's worth all the trouble. These habits focus on achieving any form of success you care to establish and the steps to get there. The first three habits cover elements of accountability and then how you'll need to hold yourself accountable or take responsibility for your results. The good news? You may feel that the success you desire lies in someone else's hands, but in fact, you will learn that you are the one that can make it happen.

- Be Clear (Not Just In Your Own Head)
- Teach Them To Fish For Solutions (Don't Solve Their Problems)
- Take Responsibility (Stop Blaming)

The next three habits reflect the many benefits of creating autonomy for your team and the leadership behaviors you'll need to foster that kind of autonomy. Most leaders are largely unaware of the importance of creating autonomy for their team, even though they're personally motivated by its benefits. We'll look at the choices you can make under various circumstances to ensure you know what type of help is needed by your team and when.

- Let Go (Responsibly)
- Motivate More (Help Less)
- Level Your Team (Stop Training Them To Look Up)

BE CLEAR
(NOT JUST IN YOUR OWN HEAD)

Your team wants to do what you want, they just don't know what you mean. Clarity is the essential element to developing autonomous, highly engaged teams. Unclear language, expectations, behaviors, and vision are the chief stumbling blocks to the kind of leadership that will allow you to get your life back.

BE CLEAR ABOUT WHAT YOU MEAN

I've encountered leaders having lots of conversations in the workplace where no one on their team knows what they mean. Frequently, leaders believe they have given their team adequate direction, and yet the team members don't understand what the leader really means. If you want your team to be accountable and responsible, then everyone needs to know what you actually want them to do.

While building CORE, I realized that a shockingly large number of leaders don't even know exactly what *they* mean when giving direction (not every time, but often around important items). When I dig deeper, I uncover some generic thoughts like—*I want them to think ahead, to be more proactive, or to learn from their mistakes.* Such generalities aren't helpful when providing direction to a team. As I work with most of the leaders in the program, I even find that it's hard for me to understand what they're talking about.

To help leaders get clarity, I work with them to break down their laundry list of intentions by asking questions like—*What does "being proactive" look like to you? What would the team need to accomplish to "be proactive"?* During this process, leaders search their mind's eye and envision the scenario(s) they want and then share how they would describe them to their team. Then we practice what to say to their team members to help leaders understand how to get the results they want.

For example, I recently advised a leader to clarify what "proactive" meant regarding his team. He said, "Because of the mistake on the line yesterday, the team will need to figure out what they need to do so it doesn't happen again. I'd like them to meet and discuss the real root cause and then explore the changes that would stop it from recurring."

In this way, the general idea of "having a team be proactive" turned into a leader developing a very specific, clear, and concrete way to get there. I've realized through decades of work in the field that leaders need to go from their general idea to getting a clear understanding about what their team needs to hear and see in order to accomplish leadership's strategic objectives. We always stay with it so leaders can get more and more specific to find the clear meaning of what to say to their team and get the results they want—a practice that saves time and lots of headaches.

BE CLEAR ABOUT YOUR EXPECTATIONS

Between leaders using language no one can understand and then introducing philosophical ideas—like we "believe in excellence" (what the hell does that mean?)—leaders create an ambiguous atmosphere where teams don't know how to accomplish the work that needs to be done successfully. When you use clear language, your team knows exactly what you mean, and you will get the results you want. Very often, leaders in my program have the realization—*I don't know what I mean, so how will you know what I mean?* Like in the example above, the leader had an idea about "being proactive" as a concept, then had to think through and articulate the steps the team needed to accomplish to meet his expectations.

Frequently, leaders give directives and don't go over their expectations. *Come up with the plan*, might be all a team member hears, but leaders don't give them the proper time constraints or support—the how, what, when, and why around the task. Once these are clear, team members will be better able to meet the needs of their supervisor and the company.

When you want to lead, it's important to keep in mind that staff is hardwired to want to do what you want, except much of the language you use gets in the way. Teams simply don't know what you mean. I encourage teams to ask questions so they can understand confusing language or concepts that leaders sometimes use as shorthand during their busy days to quickly clarify their specific expectations. But teams shouldn't have to work so hard. That job starts with you, the leader. Even the word "accountability" can mean something different to people. So how do you help people become accountable?

> **Lack of clarity arises when there is a disconnect between our concepts and what we actually mean.**

I discovered that the original value of CORE focused on teaching a coaching style of leadership to make team members more independent. However, its value grew to incorporate so much more. One of the earliest groups to implement the basic concepts of CORE found it hugely helpful for operationalizing other major programs or philosophies, in part because they implemented this one habit and became clear—using simple and specific language to express their ideas and expectations.

BE CLEAR ABOUT THE RESULTS YOU WANT

Essentially, CORE reverse engineers the problem for leaders. We help them take the time to understand what their team needs to do differently so leaders can clearly see what they need to do differently to get that improved outcome. Instead of glossing over it, we help leaders carve out the time to get focused and think their way through the behaviors that will get them there.

As we mentioned in the last chapter, the Performance Improvement Cycle is a key way CORE helps leaders get the perspective and clarity they need to achieve their desired outcomes. In it, we talk to leaders about their challenges and the results they want. Then we reverse engineer the results to find the clearest way to communicate with teams to get those outcomes.

For example, we ask a leader,

"What's the problem you have?"

"Things aren't safe."

"What are the results you want to see?"

"Zero accidents."

"What's your desired result?"

"People aren't having accidents because they are following the safety rules."

Clear leadership drives clear team behaviors.

It seems straightforward, but when we first discuss these behaviors in CORE, leaders often have a hazy idea about how to create their teams' behaviors to get their clear outcomes and desired results. We provide the space to help leaders identify and break down the specific behaviors their team needs to achieve their vision. But identifying a team's ideal behaviors is just the beginning. Then we look at the culture the leader needs to create to make those behaviors more common and examine the leadership behaviors that will drive their teams to deliver the needed results.

Clear language speaks in behavioral terms.

It's about envisioning what kinds of behaviors you need to perform to get the right behaviors from your team. Let's look at a few examples. In the case of creating a safe working environment, a leader wants a team member to "take ownership."

For clarity, the team member will ask, "What do you mean when you say 'take ownership'?"

The leader replies, "To make a commitment and either meet the commitment, or, if you think something will come up and you can't meet the commitment, to rearrange or renegotiate the commitment."

"Treating each other with respect" is another example of a popular idea that leaders and teams want to implement. In this case, it's important to define the specific behaviors that everyone agrees show respect and work toward cultivating those behaviors. Until leaders do that, "respect" is just an idea. Yet another example could be when a leadership group says they want their team to take "shorter breaks." When I ask them what that would look like, they usually respond by saying they don't know. Then we work through the behaviors that need to occur to make "shorter breaks" a reality.

BE CLEAR ABOUT THE WHY

Clarity of vision is one of CORE's most fundamental elements. When leaders complain during the program that they have a list of things they don't like about their team, I ask a simple question, "What are you driving toward?"

This usually meets with a blank expression. Then, I ask another question, "What are you doing to get the behaviors that drive your desired result?"

Most leaders don't take the time to think about the roadmap that would drive their desired results, let alone write it down. It's very important for you to have a vision for success as a leader and help define that success for your team. The very first part of our program focuses on vision. What is your vision for success? Don't worry if you can't come up with an answer at first. Most leaders don't have a clear vision.

If you aren't clear about your vision, your team isn't either.

Clarity of vision is the beginning of having a way to achieve it. For example, when leaders get clear about their vision, they all usually talk about a happier workplace and more engaged work environments. Some are interested in improving safety and getting a quality product out on the market. Even when leaders can articulate their visions, they often stop there, and have no plan to get there. Unclear leaders are in a day-to-day grind that eats away at their personal lives. The grind doesn't create clarity. You will find clarity when you step back to get the 60,000-foot view not only of your business, but your life. Being a witness instead of always being "the doer" fosters this holistic approach.

RELATIONSHIP BUILDING IS THE NAME OF THE GAME (MASTER PERFORMANCE IMPROVEMENT CYCLING)

Our original goal was to help leaders build their skills and daily habits to coach more. However, we discovered that CORE also provided elements of accountability as a basic set of leadership skills (called the Performance Improvement Cycle), which are equally as valuable to make your vision for success a reality. Once you've decided upon your vision, the culture you want, and the results you want to achieve, then you can use the elements of the Performance Improvement Cycle—and the foundational skills that go with it—to provide the clarity leaders need to drive their desired results. When implementing the Performance Improvement Cycle's basic leadership skills in the program, it became evident that relationship building is the name of the clarity game.

Can you imagine that you hold the power to unleash the unlimited individual talents on your team and engage them just by being

clear? It sounds easy, right? Then why is ambiguity such a common problem among leaders?

Clarity is the common thread of the entire program. We build leadership skills to set clear verbal expectations and also create written ones. A big chunk of our work involves rewriting roles and responsibilities with clear language. I ask questions like—*What do you want your team to do? How will you hold them accountable to achieve those results?*

Getting clear about how to get those results is one part of the process; another is to follow up and then support the team to help them deliver and discover ways for them to be accountable. Support involves getting the team the resources and skills they need to achieve those results and making sure we set them up for success. If any of those steps are missing—unclear follow-up to verify the team is doing the behaviors necessary to drive desired outcomes, or lack of support—then the leader has not held the team accountable. This gap in the cycle leaves the leader believing there isn't a way to accomplish their vision.

At the heart of the six habits is the Performance Improvement Cycle—set expectations, train, coach, provide feedback, use positive reinforcement to drive the right behaviors. The fundamental skills that support the cycle include open-ended questions, listening effectively, identifying specific behaviors, managing emotions, and understanding others or removing judgments.

Every step of the cycle is a well-known element. However, the program found that we needed to turn this into a repeatable model that leaders could use as a go-to while creating sustainable changes that achieve exponential success. During the program, leaders learn how to keep repeating the cycle through our action learning projects, which bring these kinds of transformational changes to life.

How do you set your team up for success?

Say people are taking half-hour breaks when they only get fifteen minutes. Every problem like that has a cycle that can be worked through where most of the steps need to be applied at every level of the problem. For example, if a leader recognizes a broken attendance program and they want to fix it, they have to get the senior team to set that expectation and then cycle through all the stages—train, coach, provide feedback, recognize the right behaviors to motivate, and use positive reinforcement to drive the right behaviors.

The whole cycle needs to be implemented and done at the right level to create a sustainable change. Each level of leadership has to be held accountable for what's appropriate at their level to affect the change. So if you are the plant manager, you'd have a very different set of expectations than if you're the supervisor holding a frontline person accountable when they return from break.

The Performance Improvement Cycle eliminates assumptions and helps clarify your vision. We focus on things like—*What are your challenges in setting expectations? What are your training challenges? What are your coaching challenges? What are your feedback challenges?* Over and over again, we stamp out assumptions and get clear on a leader's strategic goals and objectives. Assumptions can form our vision and blur it too. Talking openly about assumptions through open-ended questions helps to remove them and clarify meaning.

The Performance Improvement Cycle is where the rubber hits the road to implementation. It's not just about teaching leaders to coach their team members to become more independent through clarity, autonomy, and accountability, but also how to implement specific behaviors that breathe life into the leader's vision.

Whether a CEO is interested in implementing various concepts or theories; or the head of the maintenance department wants shorter break times; or a manager of the line wants to make sure safety policies are being followed—the performance cycle is how leaders and teams learn how to do all the things that need to get done. **Without the application of most of the performance cycle, organizations in these scenarios accomplish some things but never enough to achieve a sustainable impact.** Eighty to ninety percent of every group has the same response when we ask them about their performance gap—what they are seeing from their teams versus what they wish they saw. Most are stuck in the gap and haven't found a way out of it.

It is the leader's first and foremost initial responsibility not to give people work they can't do.

Teams have to be set up for success with the resources to do their job, and then enough follow-up and coaching to identify and provide anything else they need. But leading to live isn't just about logistics—you have to own your outcomes and drive what you want to see. You have to know that you can make it happen. Teaching people to fish for solutions is one way to get that confidence and is the second leadership habit necessary to achieve exponential success so you can lead and enjoy your life more.

TEACH THEM TO FISH FOR SOLUTIONS
(DON'T SOLVE THEIR PROBLEMS)

Leaders usually help their team solve their problems, or more often take the problem on as their own. Instead, we invite leaders to disrupt that dynamic—**asking them to teach their team members how to fish for their own solutions.**

Until individuals learn to solve their own problems and take responsibility for solving those problems, they will always look to their leader for solutions and stay dependent. Teaching team members how to find their own solutions is the underlying way to bring independence to team members. But solving team members' problems is a hard pattern to break because leaders love solving their teams' problems. Essentially, feeding them fish (solutions) also feeds a leader's need to be needed.

Coaching team members to be more independent changes the internal wiring of a leader.

It feels good to be valuable. And it may even feel threatening to get out of the fish feeding (problem-solving) routine—if team members learn how to fish for solutions, will they need their leader? The answer is definitely yes. Once team members find their own solutions, leaders are free to think strategically. Other leaders might feel it's more time-efficient to solve their teams' problems or do things for them. But in the long run, it actually wastes time to keep problem-solving rather than helping them discover solutions on their own.

WHY IS THIS IDEA SO DISRUPTIVE?

Not only do I ask leaders to withhold that good feeling of being valuable, but I also ask them to interact less with their team. People need space to learn to fish for themselves. And when they do, they need less guidance to achieve better results. This means that turning a leader into more of a coach involves delayed gratification. It's a sea change from the traditional leadership style. Once fish are being caught by team members, leaders then have time to think and implement their strategic directives, bringing the company light years closer to their goals and missions.

So instead of a boss saying to themselves, *Feed them solutions to their problems, feed my team, feed my team*, the shift in the leadership thought process becomes, ***Teach them to fish for solutions, teach them to fish, teach them to fish.*** This concept counters everything we've ever told or expected leaders to accomplish, gives leaders a new purpose, and puts what they need to do to be good leaders into sharp focus. Teaching your team members how to find their own solutions involves a change in mindsets, feeling sets, and internal wiring of the typical leader. **How much better will it be for team members when they can fish for themselves? The possibilities for discovering quality solutions that are easier to execute are more plentiful.**

SO WHAT DOES A LEADER HAVE TO DO TO CHANGE FROM FEEDING TO TEACHING?

As we learned earlier, leaders get "stuck" in what they see as the value of being helpful. Feeding people solutions feels good on a lot of levels. When a leader is the helper or the feeder, so to speak, there's a warm, nurturing feeling that goes along with being the provider and "problem-solver." A feeling similar to the gratification parents feel when they take care of their children. But as all parents know, encouraging that kind of dependence isn't helpful. When a leader stops solving their team's problems and instead coaches them on how to fish for their own solutions, the leader ends up not being needed in the traditional way anymore, just like empty nesters. During my program, leaders develop the awareness they need to transition from what has felt good in the past into a behavior that might not feel as good initially, but is a better idea overall.

Seeing team members accomplish more with less involvement can be surprising. During a recent session, a participant shared that his team had found a problem and put together their own set of solutions, but they almost didn't tell him. The discovery took him aback. Then he realized he wanted that exact outcome—his team found a problem and solved it their own way. Ideally, when it works well, the leader doesn't get into the weeds of team members' problems anymore. The leader might not even know a problem needs addressing.

Once teams reach this mastery, leaders understand that their team members don't "need" them so much—a fact that is as absolutely empowering as it is terrifying. However, it gives leaders the tools to make big shifts in the way they spend their time. Teams will appreciate using their skills and talents to solve problems in a way that will pleasantly surprise their leaders when they get the opportunity.

THEN HOW DO LEADERS FEEL VALUABLE?

When leaders become more strategic, their value comes from being able to do work with a higher impact. This changes the way they get their needs met. Instead of thinking *team members need me a lot*, they think *I have more impact*. Leaders eventually replace the joy of helping with the joy of making important strategic decisions.

Leaders need to learn how to have a new kind of joy. To do so, they have to shift their motivation, which is internal transformational work (not training) and much more than a behavioral shift. It's not about whether a leader knows how to teach their team how to fish, but whether a leader would choose to teach them how to fish. We created CORE to address these community challenges by helping leaders share their feelings, in order to better help them through that internal shift, rather than trying to change their internal wiring on their own.

The more leaders open up about their feelings, the easier the transition to coaching becomes. This is likely because everyone finds comfort and feels joy differently, has similar challenges when teaching people how to fish, and might miss the old way of leading. When leaders understand they aren't the only ones being challenged by this new coaching leadership style, as a group, they become more willing to let go of feeding solutions to their team.

However, when leaders don't share their experiences, organizations get stuck in their ability to coach teams to find their own solutions, leaving their teams dependent on them. The next chapter further explores leadership accountability and the need to ensure that leaders receive sufficient support and training so they can successfully fulfill their roles.

TAKE RESPONSIBILITY
(STOP BLAMING)

I've seen people blamed and even fired over things that are not their fault. Blaming leaders who don't have enough skills doesn't make sense either. Good leadership is all about making sure we don't ask people to do things we never trained them to do. **We show respect for people when we make sure leaders can do their job and give them the resources that help to fully support their team members.** How is it respectful to ask leaders to accomplish everything expected of them without support?

For example, let's say a company has an attendance policy based on a point system. A team member's kid could be dying of cancer, and they would get three points because it doesn't matter what's wrong—that's the policy. If they are absent, they receive three points no matter what the reason. Supervisors add up the points, and when they get high enough, that team member gets written up. This practice can deeply damage an organization's culture because people feel mistreated through discipline and improper judgment, the kinds of things people do when they don't know how to manage. Leaders can change unfair policies like these when people learn how to use their judgment and how to have a variety of critical conversations.

It takes special skills for a leader or supervisor to manage well. Typically, supervisors started off doing the same work as the people they supervise. Then, we assume that if a team member has attendance issues, the new supervisor will know how to handle that situation. They don't always handle it well. Even with a great policy in place, it doesn't mean the supervisor will know what to do. They need to be trained and coached, and probably watch someone handle the situation well before practicing it for themselves.

So often, we assume supervisors give clear expectations, good training, effective coaching, and valuable feedback—but they don't always know how or find the time to cover everything needed for great results. **Leaders often have conversations they aren't prepared for, while companies overlook their responsibility in the communication gap and let those leaders flounder.**

We have experimented with having the program include time for leaders to complete people-related, problem-solving projects, which we refer to as Action Learning Projects. While working through these projects, leaders begin to understand that it takes a lot of thoroughness, time, and attention to address any broad people-related challenge—like creating an attendance policy that isn't punitive or damaging to their culture but also addresses individuals with serious attendance issues. In a building of one thousand people, made up of one hundred leaders and nine hundred operators, there's a lot of conversation around who's absent and why. There's also a lot of judgment and assumptions, so sometimes changing a point-based attendance policy doesn't come easily. But even if HR rewrote the policy, it wouldn't work without the supervisors completing the program and taking the time to practice having critical conversations, a key way we can truly know people and allow them to contribute fully.

ALLOW PEOPLE TO CONTRIBUTE TO THEIR FULL POTENTIAL

By allowing people to contribute their full potential, leadership creates a path for team members to be more fully who they are and to better understand what drives them personally. This helps them grow profoundly and leads them to take on more responsibility, instead of always trying to complete a to-do list given to them by others.

The value people create by living to their full potential is limitless.

This kind of evolution is not a nebulous, "woo-woo" idea about team building. It's not about a kinder, gentler society. This is a profound shift in the way people do business when team members show up authentically and are able to solve their own problems. It's about taking the traditional model and turning it on its head. It's also something that isn't absorbed by simply reading my books on the subject in one afternoon.

Creating coaches takes time and is more of an evolution, involving a dedicated commitment by a leader to set clear expectations, ensure proper training, coach effectively, provide feedback from the heart, and strategically use recognition to drive behavior—all skills that can only be established over the long term.

When an HR person with at least ten years' experience gets called into a problem in the workplace, they usually have a conversation that goes something like this—*Johnny isn't doing a good job*, or *I don't like Susie*. Then the HR person will ask about the expectations—*What have we done to help Johnny? Have we trained Susie? Was there any clarity regarding the problem? Has there been any coaching, feedback, or support?* Typically, the leader won't pass that test.

Coaching your team members to be more independent takes apart that repetitive, unhelpful cycle and bridges that gap in leadership. It begins by identifying some overwhelming expectations:

- Whose responsibility is it to make sure we have clearly set expectations?
- Whose responsibility is it to make sure we have fully trained people?
- Whose responsibility is coaching and feedback?
- Whose responsibility is it to make sure they recognize the things people are doing right so they know what to do more of?

When we understand what is our responsibility and what is our team's responsibility, then we are better able to recognize unreasonable expectations that often are at the heart of blaming.

LEADERSHIP SKILLS NEED TO BE SUPPORTED

If supervisors aren't skilled in having these conversations, there shouldn't be a policy in place requiring them to do so. For example, if we ask someone to bake cookies, we know it takes a certain amount of time and skill working with some equipment, along with preventative maintenance. **However, when it comes to leadership, there's usually**

an attitude that *it's something people should just know.* **Trust me. They don't know.**

Sure, some people are naturally gifted leaders, maybe ten to twenty percent, but the rest are just leaders doing the best they can. They are communicating the way their parents or managers have talked to them in the past. For example, if a supervisor had some fairly tough leaders, they would use the same tone. Doing the best they can often means mimicking a situation they've experienced. Until they take the program, they don't have any other reference.

I've learned in all my years of experience with this work that leaders have a really tough job. There's a lot of pressure in the middle—I mean a lot. Customers, senior-level leaders, and plant managers all crack the whip. They're in a vice, and that isn't right—*Here's the problem, you have to fix this* is most likely what they hear on a daily basis.

Whether the buildings have a leak, there are not enough people, or missing parts need to be found, problems frequently come at mid-level supervisors from all directions. Then, they instruct their team to go fix the problem with a requisite list of things to do. If the team doesn't perform, their supervisor ends up getting caught in the middle and taking a lot of heat. It's like a server at a restaurant who has to deal with customers, bosses, and cooks all complaining when they're just trying to serve the food. They're doing the best they can to get through the shift.

One company I worked with had a senior leader who would come into the facility on a regular basis and point out all the things he didn't like to his supervisors. What good does that do for anybody, especially company morale? Every time a supervisor turned around, there was something else they weren't doing right. They faced so much criticism. The only way to change the situation involved changing that trajectory, so I suggested that the senior leader come in the next day and give the supervisors a list of the ten things that are going right. People will see what you reinforce.

Someone can't give something they don't get. When a person is under-cared for and under-supported, they can't take great care of other people. Instead, they're empty, worried, anxious, cornered, and they feel alone. Once leaders get the support they need, they can create team members who are more independent, which creates a community that can transform companies. In the fourth habit, Let Go (Responsibly), you will learn how to manage the kinds of worries and fears that can frequently come with leadership.

LET GO
(RESPONSIBLY)

Letting go responsibly means trusting things will work out even when there is fear or worry that they won't. It's a process that involves releasing control and leaning into a feeling of surrender instead of worry or fear. Sometimes organizations pursuing a strategy of empowering teams to do more believe it will be an easygoing process. They think leaders will simply let their teams solve problems and make decisions. But there isn't anything simple or easy about that process for some leaders, especially ones who want and need to be in control all the time.

When leaders learn how to let go, team members become more independent.

For a large portion of the leadership community, letting go is a problem. But they rarely realize their greatest fear—team members seldom "break" anything. I constantly have to remind leaders, *What could your team break?* The truth often helps them understand that it's safe to let go. Usually, leaders begin by allowing teams to handle things that don't freak them out, like organizing a party. Then they work up to letting their team members make bigger decisions. Over time, leaders need to get used to continually broadening the responsibilities they delegate until surrendering control becomes normal. Progress begins with a leader's awareness that they may want to control things, but choose to let go instead.

A while ago, I talked to a group of leaders and asked them what was going right with their leadership. Three out of ten leaders there talked about how the things going right had nothing to do with them. They said their team got "x" done, and they could get "x" done because they weren't in the way. I told the group that was a sign that we were on the right path. Over time, letting go should sound like teams getting things done without their supervisor's involvement.

WHAT DO YOUR TEAM MEMBERS DO INDEPENDENTLY?

Letting go of trying to control team members is about believing they will come up with better solutions on their own, while giving them the space and resources to get there. No leader ever micromanaged or worried their way to great leadership. When teams get things done without their leader's involvement, they've developed confident, able team members. Yet when I talk to leaders, they're concerned about claiming their team's successes as their own.

When the focus is on their team's success, leaders have a big hidden fear that somehow they will appear to be trying to own their team's work— or worse, point out that the organization doesn't really need them.

Leaders with this mindset don't understand that while they may only be the spokesperson for their team's accomplishments, leadership allows their team to get those results. It is completely appropriate that leaders speak about their team's problem-solving skills, whether they fixed a machine or met a major goal.

This isn't about a leader taking credit for other people's work or singing their own praises. It's a simple statement of fact that leadership is going right, highlighting their team's development and ability to solve problems independently. **The practice of a leader broadcasting their team's accomplishments—which are not their own and they had nothing to do with—needs to become a desirable trait of leadership.**

Companies keep saying this coaching style of leadership is what they want, but there isn't a very clear policy to that effect, one that might encourage the following—*Come and tell us what your group did without you. What did you let go of this week? And what did that look like?* An accomplished leader lets their team run an entire presentation without them. But some leaders don't recognize that or are afraid of what might happen if they're perceived to be irrelevant. They believe they should always speak for their team. Leaders who resist letting the team speak for themselves are stuck in the idea that they should be the front person. The thinking goes that they are being paid to lead their team, and it should be clear that they are in charge and therefore need to be seen.

GET USED TO THE IDEA OF NOT ALWAYS BEING FRONT AND CENTER

The first stage of letting go means giving up the idea of being the chief decision-maker. Your mindset will shift to appropriately delegating responsibilities to other team members. It's about truly moving away from a set of ingrained ideas and mindsets to a completely different, more inclusive one. Because some leaders think this is risky, they tell me they have to make sure the organization has caught up to this idea before they get on board with this kind of shift.

Leaders fear a clash of old and new leadership in this first step. However, clarity always takes away fear. They need to understand the signals they receive from higher-level management. Are they saying that leaders should be the problem-solvers? Are they getting the message that their team needs to speak for itself? Are they getting a message for team members to become more independent or not? For companies that keep saying they want this kind of coaching style of leadership, leaders often question whether the organization is saying one thing and doing another in holding leadership accountable.

For instance, many people might be in a bonus program, or have a performance review that asks about their accomplishments—meaning when there is a problem, how does the leader fix it? Recently, a woman told me she got dinged on an internal job interview because she spoke too much about what her team accomplished and not enough about what she did. Once that was called out as a reason she didn't get the job, she assumed they didn't want independent team members, and she had better be able to show what she does on the job. That kind of pushback in her internal interview flies in the face of a more coaching style of leadership, one that values the team's accomplishments as proof of her successful leadership.

She could have clearly said that she developed her team, taught them skills, and created the infrastructures to support them so they could solve important problems. The woman is a relatively young leader and took her feedback to mean that the organization wanted her to release control over her team, but they didn't really mean that. Day in and day out, leaders spend time monitoring the environment of their organization, trying to figure out what they actually mean, when that time could be better spent on strategic planning.

Keeping Your Cool Under Duress

An important example where leaders learned to trust involved a plant's central motor shutting down—a big motor—the kind that when it goes out, streets need to be closed. Suddenly, the plant couldn't supply people with what they normally received. A big issue concerned who would get what, since nobody seemed to get what they wanted. Contracts were involved, along with many serious logistical issues. The higher-ups knew they couldn't figure out a solution efficiently, so they put the team responsible for solving the problem in a room.

The plant firmly believed in the principles of coaching their team members to be independent. Senior executives asked the team to come up with what they thought should happen and how they would handle it. I remember that group. I witnessed how much confidence leaders built in their team members when they were being trusted by leadership to come up with a good solution to an enormous problem—and they did. But I also remember thinking that this was the last place most leaders go—to trust their team enough to find a way out. Leadership recognized that they couldn't solve the problem and stayed away from the trap of micromanaging the team's solution.

I have seen many examples of how senior leaders, especially when under duress, went the other way and took back total control. In my experience, I would often see supervisors ask for input, but still have their hands in the cookie dough. The pandemic was an example of how many times leaders under stress were too worried to let go. They had everything to lose, and the pandemic was undoubtedly as big a problem as they'd ever faced. The more afraid they were, the more they micromanaged.

Letting go is really about dealing with fear.

What do you do when the going gets tough? Sure, many situations can make us afraid. But as I mentioned in the last habit, Take Responsibility (Stop Blaming), we need to understand how to respond instead of reacting to the fear. During the pandemic, for example, leaders reacted by putting shortsighted policies in place, which made it difficult to pivot when the crisis waned. This fear led to a slow response during shifts in employee lifestyles and/or expectations after so many had worked from home, as evidenced by the "Great Resignation."

However, this would have been the best time to turn the reins over to their teams to figure out what to do and how to meet their own needs. And yet, that was the least likely thing leaders considered. Their reactionary mindset became, *Oh, we just have to settle this. It's a crisis. So we'll have to make some decisions and some policy changes.* They defaulted to their comfort zone and went very top-down in their leadership style.

Challenges Awaken Comfort Zones

My hope is that organizations looking for a coaching style of leadership would realize their reactionary behavior in times of crisis. They would note how challenges awaken comfort zones, and the cure is to stop the cycle of reaction during these times by letting go. **I hope leaders will understand that just as letting go works during everyday decision-making, they will also trust the process to be the best way to handle tough circumstances.**

This stage of letting go came up with colleagues during my engagement survey work. I am a big proponent of having this kind of survey completed by employees, not by leadership. When leaders organize engagement or satisfaction surveys, they usually build them on the foundation that whatever goes right or wrong is because of leadership. So if a team member needs something fixed, they need to complain to leadership, and they will take care of the problem.

The idea that a leader can fix everything for their team just isn't true.

Engagement surveys run by leadership, analyzed by leadership, and resolved by leadership are part of the problem. This is because it feeds the unrealistic idea that organizations expect leaders to solve every problem. But, when teams of employees look at the results of the surveys, they take responsibility for whatever is discovered, handle the feedback themselves, and decide what to do about the problems. That exercise builds maturity that is much more profound than teams having a vested interest in outcomes. It's more like a complete mindset shift for leaders and their teams.

BECOME FOCUSED ON GROWING YOUR PEOPLE

The second stage of letting go educates people to communicate in a way that fosters successful team independence.

- What is the problem we want to solve?
- What don't we know that we need to know?
- What would it take to get that information?
- How would we organize that?
- What steps would we take?

No small group of leadership members can take care of every situation. Problems in an organization don't get solved that way. As we shift responsibility for success to all of us, teams understand there's no one else but them with the authority to take care of the team and their work. More than just team members with a vested interest in successful solutions, this type of education actually shifts their mindset, as team members feel they are in charge of what they need and how to get it.

It feels more like ownership than simple participation.

Leaders who have been able to share this type of education among their team members see a powerful shift in their perspective. Teams leave behind the idea that leadership is to be blamed when things go wrong and stop expecting them to fix problems. Instead, they move toward identifying problems and coming up with their own solutions.

One of the most common complaints in every engagement survey involves teams' dissatisfaction with the way leaders communicate. In response to the survey results, leaders react to the negative feedback, guess at what needs to change, and the survey results repeat. I have found a process that works so much better. Teams of employees review the results, establish what better communication would look like, and participate in making the changes. When team members experience getting their needs met, they no longer expect leadership to have all the answers.

In fact, one of the most memorable examples of this led a senior leader to comment, "I watched the employees shift before my very eyes into independent thinkers."

> **When leaders let go, their team learns the lessons they need, appreciates their own ability to control things, and understands how to fix things they don't like.**

The idea of letting go ties into the organization's realistic expectations of its leaders. Certainly, the core vision of a company isn't something that eight people in a room can accomplish alone. If everyone is executing the vision, everyone needs to participate in decisions.

- Identify what is and isn't working
- Consider what they think would be better
- Propose the changes that need to be made
- Make those changes on their own (if out of scope, consult with someone else)

This way of thinking is a profound shift for teams steeped in hierarchical leadership. But in reality, those bullet points are simple in practice. It boils down to team members being more aware and action-oriented.

This solutions-based approach helps dependent team members stop focusing on the problem. Since some teams expect someone else to solve the problem, they get stuck on the problem instead of creating solutions. A leader's choice to let go empowers their team members to take ownership of problems. But building this type of community takes time and energy, which can exhaust leaders. One leader even asked me if I had a magic wand they could just wave. When leaders and teams realize there isn't a magic wand, they stop blaming—even if the process leading to independence isn't entirely smooth.

IMPLEMENT YOUR TEAM'S IDEAS

The third stage of letting go is about implementing the ideas of the team. Stages one and two are more leadership-oriented, yet introduce the power of the team. In stages three and four, the team leads results-driven problem-solving. During step three, a leader often has to give up perfectionist ideals for the occasionally bumpy road of team independence.

When things don't work out exactly as the leader would have envisioned, the up-and-down journey to their team's independence might discourage them. But even the low points can teach leaders to understand that when they try something new—like a coaching style of leadership—frustration doesn't always lead to discouragement. It can lead to major breakthroughs that unleash their team's talents and abilities.

Why do so many organizations get stuck in the implementation phase? During my many years of working with leaders, I've been surprised (if not disappointed) that so many neglect to implement their team's ideas. When I reflected on plausible reasons, I discovered many leaders had the attitude, *it's always been this way, so why change it now?* And other leaders see new ideas as too risky, but the actual risk lies in not implementing the ideas from the people closest to the work.

Along my journey, the work of Alan G. Robinson and Dean M. Schroeder, authors of *The Idea-Driven Organization*, had a profound impact on the way I saw this more clearly. In all my years of continuous improvement, I'd always believed that teams need to implement their ideas, not just come up with them. Alan reinforced this thought in a much more clear and powerful way. His research has shown that teams achieve effective results when leaders relinquish control of implementation.

I'll never forget the time I asked Alan how this idea compared with suggestion programs. He shrugged, saying that his way was nothing like a suggestion program. I laughed, thinking how many companies still considered "suggestion boxes" the best way to create engagement and involvement. Many organizations allow people to contribute their ideas, but haven't developed the capabilities and processes necessary for proper implementation.

SUPPORT AND TRUST YOUR TEAM WILL SUCCEED

The fourth stage of letting go involves supporting the team. Leaders put processes in place to help teams accomplish their solutions independently. Rather than self-management, this approach broadens the way teams implement their own solutions and handle a range of responsibilities. The process goes something like this—leaders give the team input, identify the resources they have to work with (such as how much money they can spend), and define the required output by year's end. Then, it is up to the team to figure out how to get results and accomplish the task. In this stage, it's important for leaders to keep in mind what their Emerald City looks like and aim toward that vision. What do leaders and their teams want to accomplish together?

There are a few guardrails when implementing team members' ideas. First, leadership has to believe that the team can implement their ideas while giving them the necessary resources and support. Second, selection of the best idea is another area where leaders need to nurture the team. If leadership decides which ideas are good and implements them, it's not encouraging an independent workforce. The team must come up with the solution and have the power to select the correct one in order to create the process for execution and implementation.

Ownership creates independent team members.

I enjoyed working with a company that took their departments from complete dependence to total independence. They introduced four stages of development—involve, educate, implement, and support. In doing so, each leader developed their team through the maturity required to work independently of management. Some issues they worked on included:

- What would the group need to know to become more independent?
- How can we teach team members what things cost so they can make informed recommendations?
- What type of training will be needed for team members to understand the implications of the increasingly complex decisions they will eventually make?

When one leader decides everything, there is only one person calling the shots. But when the team becomes independent, leaders naturally allow them to solve their own problems. Bringing teams together constructively usually involves the creation of ground rules and policies in order to help them figure out situations that used to be decided by leadership. This is the way hierarchy gives way to teamwork.

Leaders have to let go of the idea that they're in charge, and instead work to unleash the talents and abilities of their team members to solve problems.

This concept tends to sneak up on leaders because they almost always think their team needs something from them when they don't. And somehow they end up propelling themselves further into this common leadership dynamic, eventually becoming more mired in the idea *they need me*, which also ends up wasting the talents of their team members. As a result, a natural pattern develops around requests made by the team, and the need for the leader to always accommodate their requests.

Teams may keep telling their leaders that they need certain tasks accomplished because they want them to take responsibility for their actions, take the risk, and give them answers. By facilitating these requests, leaders reinforce a kind of "needy" behavior from their team, which sucks time away from their own essential, strategic tasks. It also causes team members to not live up to their own problem-solving potential and stifles the development of valuable skills and talents.

A perfect example of this kind of dependent behavior happened at one of my speaking engagements. I had asked the woman facilitating the meeting if we could spend the next fifteen minutes doing the next thing or not. Then the attendees all looked at her and asked what she thought. She said she didn't know.

At this point, one participant looked at her and said, "You're in charge. We trust you."

Right away, the facilitator figured out that we had six minutes for the next topic. She knew what she thought, but needed somebody to let her know she could make that decision about what we did next. Otherwise, a ten-person consensus would have been necessary for the simple scheduling decision about how to spend those fifteen minutes.

As leaders, we need to live in a world where we believe our team can make good decisions, or we will continually second-guess them or hover over their decisions. If we believe they do make good decisions, then a majority of team member requests, such as creating schedules and making rules, aren't things that leaders need to accomplish.

> **It is important to take the leadership relationship from a parent to a child, and turn it in to one of an adult to an adult.**

When parents have babies, they are needed in order for their babies to survive. But as their children grow older, they don't need parents to cut up their food. They may still need their parents to do the grocery shopping, but the parental role requires less responsibility for the child so they can grow into healthy, productive adults. Hopefully, by the time they're teenagers, parents can leave them alone in the house, and by the time their eighteen-year-old leaves the house, they can support themselves.

What happens when parents keep doing a bunch of stuff for kids when they shouldn't? They don't grow up and take responsibility for their lives until they're thirty (maybe never) because they aren't sure they have the abilities. This isn't doing them any favors. It's the same way in the workplace—convincing people that someone else has to take care of them is not doing them any favors.

STOPPING THE CYCLE OF DEPENDENCE

We often find examples all around that remind us to let our intuition or "gut instincts" guide us. Dorothy in *The Wizard of Oz* similarly found, at the end of the yellow brick road, that she had the power to go back home to Kansas the entire time by simply clicking the heels of her ruby slippers together. And leaders have this same inherent ability—to turn dependent team members into independent ones who can solve problems, take risks, and contribute their skills and insights.

It's not complicated. Trust is leadership's superpower.

Only leaders know the capability of their team members. They know when a team member asks them to do something if that person can do it for themselves. When leaders invest time into understanding these capabilities and giving time and space for their practice, then it becomes easier to trust which requests need action and those better left for the team. When leaders trust their team and think the best of them, there's more time to actually lead and even more time to actually live.

.

MOTIVATE MORE
(HELP LESS)

Leaders rarely check their impulse to grease the wheels of their team. Helping is in their DNA. Most leaders hear requests for help, then get on the problem-solving hamster wheel. The entire structure of the workplace involves leaders doing a bunch of things for their team members that are actually unnecessary. When their team requests help, leaders need to question (ten times more often)—*do they **really** need my help?*

As the gatekeepers of their own time, leaders have to decide when to let team members through that gate so they can take control of their greatest asset.

CORE basically teaches that there isn't one way to lead. Supervisors lead differently based on the situation. It's a concept that dates back to the eighties, which focused on creating a more independent workforce. Basically, the dynamic works through leadership styles that are less and less directive (where leaders tell their team what to do), eventually evolving into leadership that coaches—only giving direction in certain situations. What drives the coaching process? Motivating a team instead of always helping the team. Let's look at the process of how to motivate through a coaching style of leadership.

FIND OUT WHAT YOUR TEAM NEEDS

How leaders gauge their team or an individual team member makes all the difference. The best way to discover where team members stand is to have conversations about their experiences as they move toward independence. **The leader and team member must both work toward independence and communicate about the path to achieving it.** When dealing with a brand-new employee, a leader will be very directive because the team member doesn't know the ropes. Then one day, the leader can release direction because the team member has more knowledge and capability. As the team evolves, leadership will understand that team members grow in their capacity to do more than is asked of them.

Leaders need to be very clear about how to shift into this more independent model by defining their expectations. As we touched on before, clarity fast-tracks independent team members. Providing this kind of clarity focuses on managing by results rather than *the how* (the process). So, if leaders tell their team what the endgame is, they need to let the team get there themselves.

> Real damage happens when leaders do things for people needlessly—they interrupt the team's own sense of mastery, learning, and autonomy.

MOTIVATION STARTS WITH SELF-DETERMINATION

The Self-Determination Theory (SDT) considers motivation, energy directed at a goal, which defines our lifestyle choices and the ability to make long-lasting changes needed to maintain them. This model points out that understanding autonomy, mastery, and learning motivates humans. When we create workplaces that damage them, we create disengagement.

Peter Hines, a colleague of mine and author of many books on the subject, likes to say that people don't come into the workplace disengaged. They are at their peak engagement the day they start. So when they become disconnected, the question leaders have to ask is—*What did I do to cause this?* **People don't become accidentally disengaged.**

Self-determination theory suggests that all humans have three basic psychological needs—autonomy, competence, and relatedness—that underlie growth and development.

Autonomy refers to feeling one has choice and is willingly endorsing one's behavior. The opposite experience is feeling compelled or controlled in one's behavior.

Competence refers to the experience of mastery and being effective in one's activity.

Relatedness refers to the need to feel connected and a sense of belongingness with others.

"Self-Determination Theory,"
University of Rochester Medical Center

Automatically doing everything your team asks, without questioning whether it's in their best interest, will ultimately disengage them from the process of their self-determination. People are hardwired to want to be independent, unless leadership has trained them into dependency through the work environment. **In leadership, there isn't a very clear understanding about the damage done when leaders do everything the team asks.**

UTILIZE PEOPLE'S NATURAL MOTIVATIONS

If we ask people to name three things they've liked in their work life and three things they didn't, we'll almost always find the things they haven't liked were experiences that touch on isolation, traction (meaning they couldn't master something and felt unsuccessful at a task), and micromanagement. These are all areas where someone tried to control them in ways they didn't need. That will make almost anybody miserable. I call this "working against the grain."

When we work with the grain, we better understand how people think and feel—then we're able to propel them forward by responding to what they naturally need.

I don't think most leaders have any real background or working knowledge about what team members actually need to motivate them. But getting that understanding isn't complicated. Having simple, direct conversations about these topics does a lot to create leadership that fosters independent team members.

Early ideas of motivation simply suggested that you either have it (you are motivated) or you don't (you are not motivated, or unmotivated). However, more than forty years of research has shown that motivation is much more complex than this. The quality of motivation (autonomous or controlled) is key to both satisfaction and sustained success in achieving one's goals.

"Self-Determination Theory," University of Rochester Medical Center

Essentially, once these conversations take place, leaders need to let their team members practice creating their own solutions and using their own set of unique skills. But, lots of times leaders are busy with schedules full of meetings, etc. Still, things need to get done—even though reports need to be filed, and leadership may be short-staffed. It's hard for leaders to practice a new skill of trusting their team to be more independent because they're afraid something will get missed or left undone.

In this frenetic kind of energy, leaders seldom question themselves about using their time to become more thoughtful about their team's participation. For example, they might not take the time to understand that what works for one team member might not work for another. These nuances can only be realized when we slow down during the chaos of leadership to become mindful about situations, question more, and realize that the workplace structure usually drives leaders to do things for people. Just like the facilitator who couldn't clearly make the call about the number of minutes we had left on a topic—she didn't need guidance, and could make the decision herself. She just needed to get comfortable making the call.

HELP LESS BY OVERCOMING YOUR REFLEXES

Overcoming reflex responses to situations is hard—really hard. When I think about the workplace, leaders rarely expect a maturing of their team members. When the facilitator reflected on the situation caused by her participants' encouragement to make the decision about the meeting, she realized she could make that call. Pausing and reflecting is part of the practice leaders need to help their team live to their full potential. It's about making this type of reflection more or less automatic through consideration and a shift to respond, instead of reacting during a hectic day.

It's like when the doctor tests your reflexes in the exam room. He hits a spot on your knee and your leg kicks automatically. Instead of the automatic reaction—*I just do stuff for people, especially if they ask*—the response needs to reflect an awareness of your old pattern with the question—*How can I do this differently so my team can be all that they can be?* To interrupt the pattern, we need to slow down and notice our natural reactions, take the time to question them, and thoughtfully do what will benefit the team and not our old beliefs about leadership.

Steps to Shift Our Awareness and Stop the Reflex

What creates the space for this kind of shift? The first step involves an awareness of the typical (if not natural) leadership pattern to give answers or solve problems. The second shifts a reaction into a response. Leaders have to learn how to stop acting on autopilot by being fully present in order to recognize what is happening in the moment. Then, the leader rises a notch above a situation, becoming more of an observer who questions how to better support their team, instead of simply checking off to-do items. When leaders give themselves the space to do this kind of inventory, they gain a perspective about what their team does and doesn't need from them. A call that can be very tough to make without the proper support.

OFFERING FEEDBACK AND SUPPORT TO DRIVE CHANGE THAT LASTS

I have found that leaders rarely support each other in community in order to reach their leadership goals. But, the community support that leaders receive when they work my program helps them through their inevitable growing pains in this new coaching style of leadership. Feedback and support really are the only hope of driving change that lasts. It might seem like leaders reacting their way through the day is as natural as breathing. But, I've witnessed that on their quest to lead more independent teams, a leader's only source of hope is mastering these shifts. They feel ready to make the necessary, if initially uncomfortable, changes because of the support they get from other leaders on the same path.

Back to the parent analogy—they say it takes a village to raise a child, and that could not be more true. No one can do the job entirely alone. Because teachers, other parents, family, friends, neighbors, and community members surround a parent, they are better able to gauge when their child should accomplish certain things. It's the same way with leaders. They need to get the support of their community to recognize when they can release their team members into a more independent way of working. When leaders allow their team to practice their capabilities, many teams mature out of the need for leaders to do things for them. The alternative is unfortunate—if team members don't keep maturing, they get stuck, and before they know it, some have spent twenty years driving a forklift.

Growing in the job is essential for an engaged workforce. A good example of this happened when a leader in the program created one job for parts logistics, another job for parts technician, and another for sales support. The three people all worked in roughly the same area for the same business. However, in time, the leader decided to create one job for all three positions, and rotate one team member through the three functions instead. Within five to seven years, that person will be happier because the variety of jobs keeps her growing.

Once people know how to do a job, let's say after two years, that team member disengages because they have nothing else to learn. Of course, adults mature at different levels of capability while on the job. But, if leaders don't address how to grow their team, then those leaders miss an enormous opportunity to create team members who are more independent and engaged. **Leadership must create work roles that capture the way teams mature, so team members break out of childlike dependence and are free to enjoy growing into their full potential.**

HELPING LESS BREAKS THE DEPENDENCY CYCLE

So, why do leaders keep up this same disengaging routine? Many years ago, a senior leader of operations at the company literally said that he didn't think his people had the capability to do more than what leaders told them to do.

He said, "I think you guys think they have abilities they don't even have. I don't think they know how to make things that much better."

I thought, *Whoa, what? How can someone with this attitude lead a highly engaged team??* But, in my experience, this is a commonly held belief. Years ago, I did a project for the International Labor Organization—part of the United Nations—and we talked about different countries that employ people. A lot of them had a very limited view of the value workers could provide, and it got me thinking, **What must leaders really think of their team members to continue a decades-long cycle of telling them what to do?**

For twenty years, team members would need a leader to tell them what time to go on break and what time to come back, how many days the team could take off, and rules team members must follow, to name a few. All the problems that continue to happen in these businesses happen because of the attitudes of people who believe team members aren't able to do anything except their narrowly defined jobs.

People are amazingly capable—some are even geniuses—and loaded with gifts and unique talents. But the workplace has been based on the assumption that workers aren't smart or capable. Honestly, think about that for a minute. How could some companies have one thousand or more people working for them who aren't capable? When leaders underestimate the abilities of their teams, it's easy to understand how team members can sense they're being undervalued and then become disengaged.

Leaders with this negative mindset have probably had to work with team members who didn't really take on responsibility, were problematic or experienced attendance problems, and equated those struggles with people who have little to offer. These reasons can come from an assumption that team members have little going on in their lives—an assumption that causes leaders to get stuck with a false narrative about their teams' competence and capability.

And the cycle repeats as team members live out this expectation because of their leaders' treatment. This is another example of how leaders get stuck in a parent-child relationship with their workers. In the worst case, team members don't manage their own relationships, and they don't take responsibility for themselves or their work because leadership keeps more control than needed. **Coaching team members to be more independent is based on unleashing their talent, not keeping them down.**

Why do workplaces have these parent-child relationships? It's hard to say. One time, I met with a plant manager who had been implementing a more participative workplace. At that time, he spoke in a parent-child tone, proud of the fact he believed his workers could go home carefree (because he'd solved all their problems), and said something like, "I give them the ability to just concentrate on doing a good day's work, because I've gotten rid of all their problems."

So I asked him, "What would make you think that's what they need you to be doing? They're fine at solving problems. They're designed to solve problems."

What an interesting, unrealistic point of view he had. A few weeks ago, after a year in the program, he sang a different tune, "You know, I've really missed it with these people. They are very capable. We need to change how we do things." By getting closer to people's issues by conversing with his team, he understands how unrealistic and harmful his thinking had been in the past.

Many times, I think leaders get sucked into some of these gaps in culture or morale in the workplace. However, there are things that leaders can put in place to avert these patterns of behavior. By understanding how to respond to situations and communicate with their team, leaders will avoid the cultural patterns that create a dependent workforce that always looks up to leadership for their needs.

LEVEL YOUR TEAM
(STOP TRAINING THEM TO LOOK UP)

For hundreds of years, people at work have been worried about who's in charge and what they think. If a team member is constantly looking up to somebody in control, an authority-based rather than a team-based approach is at work. However, in the attendance example given earlier, effective policies can be team-based when leaders place a much stronger emphasis on team members supporting each other—the same as relating attendance to the success of the entire team. There's a huge difference between being upward-looking—*attendance is about what my boss thinks, what the boss's boss thinks, and about my role in some hierarchy*—instead of the idea that *we're a team and I care about doing our thing* without looking up a lot. **When team members are free from looking up, they have more awareness to do their job.**

LET GO TO LEAD

STRUCTURE WORKFLOWS FOR INDEPENDENCE

The way companies structure jobs, such as forklift drivers, accounts payable, clerks, operators, packers, etc., with narrow descriptions prevents the development of these positions into anything more. So, team members feel that they don't have anywhere to go and end up disengaged, especially in manufacturing. What one question could leaders ask themselves to help mitigate this kind of disengagement? How about—*how do my systems affect people in a way that hinders their development?*

> **How leaders structure work and how it flows has to be altered, and that starts with shifting systems and mindsets.**

UNDERSTAND AND PROMOTE PSYCHOLOGICAL SAFETY

One big topic concerning this type of shift is psychological safety. Timothy R. Clark, an expert in this field, talks about its phases, which go something like this—if people feel like they don't belong, then they don't feel safe enough to take risks; if they don't feel safe enough to take risks, they won't give leaders their ideas. If a leader wants their team members to be fully functioning—for example, questioning the status quo and making appropriate adjustments to remedy things they believe need to be fixed—he or she has to create a lot of psychological safety.

All of the continuous improvement results—problem-solving, engaged teams, making the world a better place, and making better products—sit on psychological safety. If leaders can make each other feel safe, create safety amongst themselves, and then create a safe workplace, they will have fertile soil for growing impactful companies capable of meeting and exceeding their visions.

But where do we begin? First, people need to feel like they belong in order to engage and prosper; this is called Inclusion Safety. The second tier, Learner Safety, is when people feel they can discover, question, and make mistakes. Eventually, people progress to the highest level of safety, Challenger Safety, where people feel safe enough to challenge the status quo.

If we don't feel safe enough to make a mistake, then we don't feel safe enough to contribute our ideas. If we don't feel safe enough to contribute, then we won't challenge the status quo. For example, one time I had an employee make a large financial mistake. When she discovered it, she waited for me to come after her. Instead, I explained that what we want to do when we make a mistake is to figure out how to learn from it. I suggested giving the solution the same amount of value as the mistake that was made. If it were a $4,000 mistake, we would spend $4,000 discovering a solution, for example. You could have knocked her over. I could tell that how I handled the situation would be important in defining how she would feel working with me in the future.

Because I didn't flare up and react, my employee felt safe enough to share what happened with an even bigger mistake. It's important to remember that when mistakes occur, maybe something bad has happened, but something constructive and important can also happen. When the even bigger mistake occurred, we examined the same issues—*What did we learn? What do we think caused it? What should we shift in our processes to make it less likely?* Now we have a better understanding of how to avoid these mistakes in the future and a better relationship due to our open communication.

HOW TO PROMOTE PSYCHOLOGICAL SAFETY

Companies can actively promote psychological safety in many ways. One of them is to make it a topic of conversation. Another is by identifying things that are troublesome—red flags to safety—then changing them. Leadership has to actively seek out things that damage psychological safety and stop those situations. Examples of this kind of harm include disciplinary procedures, write-ups, and point-factor attendance policies.

Anything that treats adults like children belittles them and erodes their trust.

As in the attendance example we talked about earlier, if your kid is sick in the hospital and you receive the same discipline as someone who skipped out on work, that is a real problem. There needs to be conversation to differentiate why people are not at work. There needs to be dialogue to better understand the nuances of situations that arise, not a one-size-fits-all kind of disciplinary system. The very use of the term "write-ups" often feels like a slap on the hand instead of honest communication in the workplace.

> People don't need to be punished. They need to be responsible to their teams and to the mission of the organization to achieve its goals. Therefore, leaders need to foster a workplace where employees are engaged in the mission and committed to being good team members.

I'll never forget the woman who worked for a company for twenty years and the hurt in her eyes after being written up for an attendance problem. I often tell leaders that they wouldn't damage their equipment that way.

We damage people when we discipline them—and the damage is often permanent. That same woman is raising a family, paying a mortgage, and making a car payment. She doesn't need to be disciplined.

Discipline came out of a fear-based traditional leadership that seeks to maintain control versus reaching employees' hearts and minds. Usually, the central issue around a person's work behavior has nothing to do with needing discipline. If people aren't coming to work regularly, they must not want to be there. There needs to be a discussion about why.

There are so many reasons people miss work. We don't need points to tell us whether someone doesn't want to work at the company. If they don't, then they can leave. But maybe the reason is something more conflicted, like a newly divorced person having a hard time with childcare who needs to modify their schedule until they get it figured out. A person shouldn't get fired over that through a disciplinary system. That kind of blunt disciplinary action is like letting people hit your equipment with a hammer.

The rebel in me has been asking this question my entire adult life— why are some leaders so comfortable treating workers the way they would never want to be treated?

I've been in environments where the entire salaried workforce doesn't track vacation or hours, but they treat the hourly population with the philosophy of maintaining control or the work won't get done. Sometimes, those same people justify this horrible attitude because they believe hourly workers are poor and uneducated. I maintain that the workplace is only responsible for creating people with horrible attitudes, not the other way around.

When leaders treat adults like children, they bring out childlike behavior in their team.

The same workplaces that are busy with disciplinary attendance policies are also the ones saying they want one hundred percent engagement and one hundred percent involvement; that their heart's desire includes people who love working at their organization. My response is always the same—if they want all of those things, quit disciplining and move toward team-based accountability amongst responsible adults.

Leadership reacts differently to the news. Some agree, but somehow they don't make it their priority to change. Some get stuck in fear. For example, leaders who can't manage without the black-and-white attendance rule manage to become powerful enough (even though they aren't really powerful) to stop the people in charge from changing their disciplinary policy—so real, meaningful change often gets shelved.

REFLECTING ON YOUR OWN MOTIVATIONS TO STAY IN CONTROL

In most workplaces, many things can hamper real change, particularly when we damage psychological safety. For example, taking team members' ideas and then putting them down. Or maybe inclusion is the issue; the team member feels like they don't belong because of the way a leader treats them. If people don't feel like part of the team, they don't feel safe to be themselves. So instead of expressing their opinion, they become closed off and guarded. Leaders have to create a safe place for people to unleash their talent, while not actively damaging that very talent. Real change happens when we take care and nurture this talent.

Leaders can prevent disengagement by practicing mindfulness, which involves taking a moment to pause and reflect. This kind of thoughtfulness is counterintuitive to the "getting things done" traditional leadership, with its list of everyday things to plow through. By initiating a thoughtful pause, a disruption in habitual patterns occurs.

> We regularly build reflection opportunities and planning into our leadership practicums. Before these experiences, leaders feel that reflection is probably bad for productivity. But what they come to understand is that productivity is about people and planning, not completing their lists.

Leaders need to reflect on what and how they do things. This pause is about engaging the brain without mindless movement and thinking before speaking. The path to coaching your team members to become more independent relies on this kind of reflection.

- How am I showing up?
- How am I leading?
- Am I giving my team members independence?
- Do they need me in the ways they think they do?
- Can I check that out through conversation?
- Do I never stop doing?
- How can I build a habit of reflection?
- Am I letting fear drive my decisions?

As we discussed in the previous chapter's section titled, "Helping less breaks the dependency cycle," the VP of Operations profiled thought his people weren't capable, and resisted this kind of thoughtful leadership before realizing the errors of his ways and granting his team more independence. I don't think he's alone, and the resistance he experienced involved issues of control. Control usually happens around fear and looks something like this—*If they don't need me, I won't have a job; I'm afraid they'll break something; They'll make the wrong decision; They won't know what to do; I should give them the answer; They'll be mad at me.* We could write an entire book about the fears that drive controlling leadership.

So, what is the cure for fear?

Trust is the antidote for the fears that drive dependent leadership while reinforcing equality between leadership and its teams. Uncertainty drives fear in leadership. The way to handle this is to lean into the uncertainty and believe the best in people by substituting fear-based, controlling thoughts with—*I think it will work out; It's okay to make a mistake; Nothing will break; How bad could it be?*

WE CAN'T LIVE IN LOVE AND FEAR AT THE SAME TIME TO LEAD THE WAY WE WANT

We either lean in and trust that things will work with people, or we act to control all the things that scare us. For example, fear dictates that if you take out that punitive attendance policy, team members will stop coming to work. However, if we work on a project as a team and make it something we all care about and commit to, team members' better selves will rise to that occasion, and the attendance will be exemplary. This break from control to coaching is a major shift in mindset that needs internal work and continual practice to change.

We literally show leaders how to think about everything they do, to discern whether they are coming from a place of fear or what we call love—leaning in.

"The higher up you go in an organization, the greater a leader's capacity for love must be. It's on us as leaders to grow that capacity for love within ourselves, to cultivate that love on our teams, and to release the full potential of each team member."

Renée Smith, Founder, A Human Workplace

This kind of love comes in so many forms in the workplace. Take a typical onboarding policy, for example. When an onboarding policy is done out of love, leaders look at how to care for the person on their first day of work and consider how to welcome the new hire. The focus becomes taking care of their needs and finding ways to care for them on that day. Sure, there are rules and safety issues that new hires need to know. However, under the guise of protection, some onboarding policies focus on things that might frighten people.

Protection is a word associated with fear. In my experience, leaders won't enter their "Emerald City" or create an independent workforce through approaching their team from a place of protection. Because leaders who focus on protection are fear-based, it results in "what-if" thinking like, *What if all the risks we take don't pan out this time? What if it all falls apart when I'm not in control?* These protective attitudes are similar to putting on armor. Leaders have to learn how to come out of the space of protection to create independent teams. **Just like you can't save your way to prosperity, leaders can't protect their way into the exponential value that comes with an independent workforce.**

It's like during those medical shows when the doctor teaches the intern how to put the tube down a throat or cut a chest open. That new doctor has to make the life-or-death cut. They have to learn. Similarly, leaders have to trust that their team can find a solution and that we are all going to live to tell the tale. Keep in mind, a majority of team members don't make the kinds of big decisions where things could go horribly wrong.

COACHING FOR IMPROVEMENT, NOT MANAGING

As a member of the Association for Manufacturing Excellence for the past twenty-something years, I've witnessed hundreds of companies practice the principles of coaching team members to be more independent. When I wrote my first book about Lean HR, I looked at the last fifty companies I'd visited and asked myself, *What did I learn from those companies about how they changed? What kept them together?* I found my answer, and the key to my long-standing passion for improving the conditions of people in the workplace—the glory of people coming together to solve what isn't working.

Community is vital.

HR isn't just something I do in my business life. The people I usually meet for dinner and on the weekends are all rooted in the work. We believe in continuous improvement ideas at our core, hence the name of my program. Whenever we're talking about HR, our hearts go pitter-patter, and we'll do it for the rest of our lives. We'd do it forever if we could. One of my colleagues put it best when he said, "You know, when I went down and worked with people on the floor, and I saw the lights go on, and I saw them feel better about themselves and solve problems, I wanted to do it forever!"

We've figured out that we believe in the **sacred value of humans and champion their journeys.** We know that the forklift driver can see and solve problems, understand processes, and do things well beyond driving a forklift—and that floats our boat. Seeing everyone finding and living to their potential in the workplace spills over into many other areas of their lives. That's what we do for a living. We go in and help people fulfill their workforce's potential in a workplace. I don't teach my program just so people can become more efficient. That wouldn't inspire me. It's not about making the product for less money.

> **The most success I've found in my work takes root in the idea of a community where everybody works through common, shared problems and their common goals.**

This kind of community builds relationships that can lead to planning holiday parties, or becoming active on a team that's sorting out why something may be out of whack. Once I was on a team that tried to problem-solve a big customer complaint regarding mold growing on a wrapper. The team went to town on that issue. They were born with the knowledge to solve that problem.

One thing we teach in continuous improvement is that people learn a great deal about the business processes and how their company runs. For example, the improvement of the entire production process begins with a team solving the problem by working in community. They decide what they think causes the problem, and those observations and insights change the process. Seeing that kind of community in action forever changes team members. The lights go on, and they become animated, interested, and engaged.

They feel a connection and are comfortable contributing together because what they think matters—the kinds of things everyone needs and wants in life. For a very long time, I worked in a freezer and oversaw people working at 34°F. The only thing that brought those women to work every day was who they ate lunch with. They lived for that community. That's the power of community.

PART II

BUILD THE SIX HABITS SUCCESSFULLY AND ENJOY LIFE MORE

> "You've always had the power, my dear, you just had to learn it for yourself."
>
> **Glenda, the Good Witch, *The Wizard of Oz***

This part of the book will help you get so skilled at the six habits that you will have the power to enjoy your life more. Incorporating the six habits into your leadership style in the following ways will make them second nature. Because you will be the leader you always wanted to be, you will have more time available to do the things you've always wanted to do. We talked about the fertile soil for good leadership in the last section. Think of this section like the soil you will use to grow the six habits that will turn you into the kind of leader you've always wanted to be. New habits are really hard to build successfully. The following approaches work well when building the six habits:

- Build Community
- Keep The Good Vibrations Going
- Leaders Need Drills
- Be On Your Side

BUILD COMMUNITY

It doesn't have to be lonely in leadership. When effective, it's a team effort. Building that team takes a regularly tended community, not one only forced together when there's a shared problem (which is when we typically find unity in the workplace). But, how do we get people to open up every day to become part of a community, not just during crunch time?

It's natural for people to connect when they have a common problem. However, in my experience, when given the opportunity, people enjoy sharing their insights by simply talking to each other. I facilitate that kind of dialogue by giving people the time and space to connect. The community formed as a result comes from shared feelings and experiences. The big surprise? People who work together all the time don't realize they have similar feelings.

SHARING VULNERABILITIES BUILDS COMMUNITY

Most think that they are the only ones with vulnerabilities, like doubting their leadership skills. As a result, people rarely sit down over lunch and talk about their leadership struggles. Instead, they pretend like everything is fine—*I've got it, I'm in charge, I'm getting my reports out, I'm doing what people ask of me.* They don't admit their truth. **Once there is a feeling of connection, leaders hear what's happening to other leaders and want to share their experiences too.** They are less about pretending and more about keeping it real. And in this way, people form a genuine connection, and can learn from each other about what's worked and what hasn't in leadership.

A great example of how I've seen leaders share vulnerabilities is when I have people work in pairs or small groups and then I prompt them with conversation topics. Afterward, they share what's happening with each other—the challenges their departments have, quality concerns, attendance problems, or whatever might be an issue in their experience. Over time, as the groups learn about coaching skills and practice using them in community, they begin to listen to their partner(s) in new ways. During the exercise, their partner(s) shares a problem, and the only two tools allowed in response are to ask questions and to listen. They may do nothing else for five minutes. Usually they can't do it because they still try to give advice.

It's painful to hear conversations with leaders at times because they can't get their head around simply asking questions and then listening to the answers. They find giving advice too irresistible. This illustrates the actual challenge facing people who want to learn how to coach their team members to be more independent: When they try to coach, even for a short time, they can't because it's second nature to tell people how to do something, which isn't coaching them or helping them to find their own solutions. Supervisors need to learn how to listen, instead of problem-solve. Listening is one of the most important ways to show respect.

Respecting and caring for people naturally builds community, but it doesn't mean that getting there is easy. It takes a lot of practice to change leadership styles. I spoke with a plant manager after a first-year program graduation as we began our second year of work. He told me that people struggled with the evolution of leadership at his company, saying, "We know better about how to lead, but we're still 'off' more than we're 'on.'" Because the people at his company knew how to lead better, they also knew when things weren't right. **Leaders and team members need the right tools and must set realistic expectations about what type of support people require to do their jobs.**

For example, people don't assume I should know how to fix the wiring if a machine doesn't work. Most of us aren't electricians, nor do we plan on becoming one. In leadership, though, there's an attitude that once promoted, a person should just know every aspect of how to lead. But most of us aren't born knowing how to be a good leader.

People are just human beings. Whatever we ask of them, they probably have to be taught. We need to be clear about what leaders need to learn to get the job done. And we need time to be coached (which simply means being given the opportunity to practice leadership skills), then receive feedback and reinforcement from someone who isn't the typical hierarchical leader.

Work using this kind of leadership style, called continuous improvement, creates workplaces where everyone can be a leader. The practice focuses on creating self-managed teams, ones that question:

- *Does the leader need to create the schedule?*
- *Or can the people create the schedule?*

- *Can the leader set all the policies?*
- *Or can the people set some of the policies?*

What drives the answers to these questions? Either history—the way it has always been done—or walking through the kind of fear brought about by this new leadership style. **Giving up control is one of the biggest challenges facing traditional leaders who want to grow into a coaching style of leadership.**

GET THE SUPPORT YOU NEED FROM YOUR PEERS

Consider a company that has the entire leadership team successfully building their coaching skills and style of leading. What happens when a significant portion of a company changes? The culture changes. The participants described the shift in many ways, including making it their habit to work from the heart; in other words, relationally. When asked what they would do about a problem now, they respond by talking to the person or people involved to better understand what's happening with them.

Support became home base, instead of the oddity it was before their participation in the program. Most leaders think they want good leadership skills—*I do the right thing at the right time, I give great feedback, I'm a good coach all the time.* But the most important leadership skill is to get support when needed.

One guy in the program had recently complained about a supervisor who said awful things and behaved horribly.

I asked him what he did about it.

"First of all, I let the manager who is in charge of the person handle it. I backed up and quit trying to control the situation. We've done some things, and I see improvement. He was probably under stress."

The employee started to become more empathetic with his supervisor's situation. When the employee notified the stressed supervisor's boss, he changed the working environment and the amount of support the supervisor and his team received. Guess what? Attitudes began to turn around.

People need to practice their leadership skills, but they also need to practice support. Go talk to someone.

During this same session, we focused on dealing with difficult behaviors—people who are angry, obstinate, uncooperative, and condescending. Listening first, then trying to understand what's going on with the people in question, took care of most of the behaviors. It's important to be firm, but in order to handle the situation in the best way, it's more important to get support. Good leadership isn't about never getting irritated by people. It's about getting irritated and then going to talk to your buddies to help you figure out a good approach. They will help you get through your triggers and your irritation through their support.

To reinforce the concept, I explained to the participants that I still practice as a leader. When my point of contact and I get challenged in a situation and someone bothers us, we'll talk it through and help each other figure out what we need to say. People don't miraculously step into the kinds of conversations that can solve difficult behavioral problems. But when people make a habit of getting support, then they talk to each other more, which makes this kind of supportive communication easier. And, after lots of practice, receiving this kind of support can become second nature.

> **Getting help is a sustainable habit. It feels good. You don't mind doing it because support helps you get your needs met.**

During a practice session, the guy with the stressed supervisor said, "This is really uncomfortable. I can't think of what to say. I don't really want to say what I need to say out loud. It's really awkward."

But then, after practicing for a while he said, "Well, once I said it, and talked to a person I felt comfortable with, I kept in mind that this is just practice and figured out how I might say this thing."

That's what getting support is all about. It goes from not wanting to say anything because they don't know what to say, to having a level of comfort when they practice. Then people help them figure out what to say, and how to say it. Afterward, they have the confidence to deliver the message.

In general, multiple viewpoints help in solving people issues. It's not that any one person is right, but the blend of their viewpoints is best.

For example, there's the "man in the street" who gives a very direct, no-nonsense approach. Then some people will see nuances others don't like or maybe didn't notice. Things people hadn't thought about. Because people are complex, we want a diversity of ideas. If we don't ask each other for support, we're only using singular ideas to drive our attitudes, behaviors, and decisions, which isn't likely to be best. When leaders are exposed to ideas they hadn't considered, they will develop a better way to handle the problem, creating much better outcomes.

This practice also results in leaders who generally don't get stuck in a judgment or reaction. When an angry person gets input, we have witnessed how the act of getting support helps to balance that negative energy. The person gets untriggered while sharing and begins to move into a much more neutral, nonjudgmental viewpoint. Somehow, in being exposed to a diversity of ideas, we can't actually hold the same narrow judgment. Sharing shines a light on our own judgments and assumptions. We don't see them until someone points out another reason someone may have behaved a certain way. Then there's an aha moment when an unexpected good idea keeps our thinking in check.

If there is only one takeaway you get from this book, please learn when and how to get support. Not that you need to be better somehow—a better person, never judgmental or angry, never controlling, without snap judgments or assumptions. That's not going to happen. But one thing that can keep all that in check is to get support. We help create an environment where leaders will likely go to each other when they are frustrated, judgmental, or feeling bad about a certain event. What people need to do is to go tell someone about it. I bring this about by creating some privacy and setting aside time for leaders to stop doing their jobs and simply share their biggest challenges or struggles. It's about creating a space to reflect, pause, and connect.

KEEP THE GOOD VIBRATIONS GOING

As we work with leaders in the program, we ask them what feels good. When they become aware of the good feelings they experience, they'll generally want to keep up the kind of behaviors that caused them. More good feelings encourage them to keep going down the new, yet unfamiliar, path of coaching. When those activities allow them to give up some of the extra worry and strain that comes with carrying their problems, they naturally do more of those kinds of things that will help them continue down that path. This is an example of a self-reinforcing cycle. Essentially, all the benefits cited above become self-reinforcing behaviors, which help leaders transition into a coaching style.

DO WHAT FEELS GOOD

It's really about leaders and teams leaning into what feels good, savoring those moments and being present in the joy that's in front of them, even if it's different from what they used to find rewarding.

Allowing themselves to be more present in their positive feelings ensures that they'll recognize that coaching makes them feel good. And we all like to do things that make us feel good. For example, a leader came to me and ticked off a list of the things she did, then shared a story about how great her team performed. When I asked her how that felt, she admitted she never really took the time to think about her feelings. After I drew attention to the fact that it felt pretty good to see her team succeed more independently, she recognized that helping to make her team shine pleased her. Then I reminded her to pay attention to that feeling. Her reinforcement not only came from her team excelling, but it also came from how good she felt about helping.

Reinforcement is personal.

Reinforcement works the same way in coaching as it does when we are trying to develop good habits. In the literature about the anatomy of a habit, they talk about a cue, something that will trigger people to pick up the new habit. For example, when someone wakes up and sees their workout clothes, that's their cue to exercise. The sight of workout clothes causes people to pay attention to how good they feel when they take care of their bodies. The literature also talks about the need for reinforcement, or rewards. So, if I run five miles, I can buy a new outfit, or invest in a new techie gadget that I've been wanting for my runs.

In this coaching style of leadership, we help leaders find cues and reinforcements that help new habits, and important skills evolve. As we touched on before, leaders require the same dedication as athletes to master the basics. And athletes stay highly skilled because their basics are very strong. It's about asking questions like, *if practice is the desired behavior, how does it get reinforced?*

Cues and rewards come from leaders who are clear about fostering and encouraging better developers of people. It's about saying goodbye to leaders who want all the attention on them—*I'm really good, I'm smart, I'm capable*—and welcoming leaders who focus and get pleasure from building great teams. These leaders are reinforced with things like meeting their team's needs, finding good support for them, and giving them room to solve their own problems, in addition to pay, bonuses, and feedback. Each element of the talent system needs to get rewired to reinforce and reward this different coaching style of leadership.

Over the years, leaders in the program become much more motivated by how they develop their people. It's been an interesting journey. Many who had been too controlling and micromanaging actually had some awareness of how that had negatively affected their teams. Some knew they weren't great leaders, but wanted to learn how to move the needle. When these middle-of-the-road leaders used the skills we practiced to unleash the talents of their teams, they really felt good about it.

Many times when I talk to one of these leaders, they proudly share what they've done to build their team, what new way they helped their team do something, or how they stayed in the background while the team got something done. The way these leaders keep helping their team become successful, and the excitement they experience when they do, tells me that those benefits are becoming reinforced habits. I've watched them make reminders for themselves, little cues, to keep the new way of building their team top of mind. The cues keep prompting them to remember and behave in a new way.

O.C. Tanner is a great example of this type of personal reinforcement. He sold graduation rings and pins, dedicating his life to employee recognition and compensation. His talk called "The Modern Manager" highlighted the way his company likes to develop people and is very "other" oriented. Leaders need to be fed by that. In other words, the act of developing people needs to make them feel good. When it does, those good vibrations motivate leaders, and they become devoted to the team's growth.

The leader's mission then becomes wanting to do anything within their power to help their team. For example, a supervisor will try to figure out what her team needs to learn and how she can support that learning. When a coaching leadership style takes hold, leaders give their teams opportunities or give them exposure to new situations. A lot of times, giving people a shot at trying something or being a part of something outside their normal routine helps them grow and develop their talents.

It feels good to help other people.

MAXIMIZING THE FEEL-GOOD BENEFITS

Teams are typically grateful for the opportunities. I like how the O.C. Tanner modern manager conversation focuses on retention and greater engagement, benefits of a coaching style of leadership. They note that thirty percent of all employees really don't like to talk to their bosses or their leader. But when leaders devote themselves to always being in their team's corner and going well out of their way to help employees, then they earn their trust. **Once there's trust, open communication develops organically. When employees feel good, they stay with these kinds of organizations, and the value of that retention is enormous.**

But, getting leaders to have this kind of commitment to their teams can be hard. They need reinforcements to stay dedicated even when they're too busy or distracted. O.C. Tanner said when he first told leaders that they needed to have this kind of devotion, some of them told him how very busy they were. Then they asked what Tanner didn't want them to get done so they had time to do what he asked. Tanner replied that he didn't really care and told them whatever the leaders needed to give up, give up. He wasn't kidding around and wanted his leaders to develop their people, no matter what.

O.C. Tanner is a great example of a company where leaders are all about developing others. Quality one-on-ones are common attributes of these types of relationships. It's about knowing employees personally and having their leaders express genuine care and appreciation for them as people. For example, if their child is sick, you've asked about the child and how things are going. Meetings aren't all about business, but rather making those kinds of personal connections that help employees feel safe and open to communicate. Those components must be there to have a good coaching relationship in order to develop people.

Having good communication is one thing when all is well. But when the going gets tough, things get tested. For example, organizations realize the commitment of their leadership to their new coaching style when a gigantic mistake happens, or some other stressful event occurs. Either they act on their newer behaviors without blame and learn lessons from the situation, or they revert to old shame-and-blame ways.

Leaders need to practice, reinforce, and reward CORE's systems long before a crisis to secure them as go-to habits and skills during trying times. This produces the kind of leadership that will see the organization through hard times quicker, with much better results.

But many organizations don't have their heads around making such a positive change.

Traditional management focuses on negative reinforcement and a lack of open communication. It is based on making employees do what they want. And if they don't, they will be punished. To break this punitive pattern, we focus on how to recognize the behaviors leadership wants into existence through open communication. We literally map the behaviors out and recognize them into reality. **That shift takes focus and a belief that if you can clarify your desired output and results, you can create whatever change you want.**

In CORE, we have a whole section on how leadership drives their own results. In it, leaders name what they want the team's output to be and what results they're looking for. Then, they get clear about what specific team behaviors they need to drive that result. In addition, they need to get clear about the kind of culture they want to create so those behaviors become more common. And finally, leaders become aware of the clarity they need to accomplish all of the above—the nuts and bolts of it. As they go through this process, leaders gain a sense that it's in their power to control output and results.

As leaders have a newfound sense of confidence in being able to right their own ship, they deepen connections made with their coworkers, feel closer to their leaders, and begin to not feel so alone. This kind of community building is naturally reinforcing. Earlier in the book, we talked about self-determination theory, which speaks to three core needs of people—mastery, autonomy, and community. A coaching style of leadership promotes all three. It's about getting the support the team needs for its own mastery, and helping them solve their own problems through autonomy, while building a sense of community through deepening connections.

When we talk about coaching for independence, we are talking about coaching for autonomy. There is a big link between autonomy and happiness in the workplace. Nobody likes to be micromanaged. When most people are asked about the three things that motivate their work and three things that demotivate it, the motivators usually include being good at what they do, having a purpose, and being allowed to do what they want to do. The usual demotivators include being micromanaged, being left alone without the support they need to do their job, and feeling set up to fail.

When leaders learn how to reinforce their team's motivators, the team has good feelings because their leaders are heading in a direction that makes them happy, which causes them to become more motivated. Getting teams onboard with the coaching style of leadership is integral to maximizing all its benefits.

In order to have a coaching style that is co-created between leaders and their teams, the employees need to be informed, educated, and spoken to about the very different, open relationship they will have with their leaders through coaching. We need to create workforces that are ready to be coached and help them know what to make of the changes that are happening in the organization. There's no changing a workplace unilaterally; the employees need to be told, and they also need to be aware of their part in the process.

It's important to meet every employee where they are. If we are going to redefine what kind of relationship they will have with their leaders—and if they are going to truly be peers—this will also affect the way they will speak to each other, deepening their connections. Some incredible benefits result when people reinforce each other through closer open connections in the workplace.

When leaders in the program come through the third time, their coaching and interpersonal skills not only get better, but they seem more relaxed and focused. When I meet most of the leaders, their job is managing them. They are confused and stressed, and don't think they have any other way to lead. We aren't just teaching them a coaching cycle. The program also teaches them that leaders have power over leadership. It doesn't have to run them. Once leaders learn how to set expectations and get clear about what they need to do, they begin to experience a different way to behave in their leadership roles, internally and externally.

It all begins with intention and clarity. And if the direction isn't working, leaders know the answer lies within them. Until leaders get some mastery of this concept, they will try to create results without a whole lot of clarity, and that's really hard.

But the lightbulb turns on slowly. When leaders first take the program, they just try to process what the output and results could be and spend time identifying them. Basically, they go from being confused to being less confused by becoming aware of this new direction, and how to get clear about creating the kind of results they want. This awareness enables them to experience the process more fully because they completely understand the concept.

By the third time leaders practice the basics of leadership, they have some mastery of how to become clear about their results and how to achieve them. Awakening to these goals and possibilities is a slow journey, and there are no shortcuts. Even after several repetitions, leaders still don't know it cold, but they have more mastery and experience, which helps them recognize how to stay focused. Knowing that leadership starts with them isn't a new feeling or idea. **We simply help leaders gain the clarity they need to create and do the things they can to drive results.**

FEEL-GOOD LEADERSHIP 101

Why are leaders so confused? Why is it such a challenge for leaders to get clear about their goals and results? Is it due to resistance or fear? My sense is that we just don't train leaders to lead very well. We don't give them much information. I think there's generally a sense that people can intuit leadership skills, and they don't need the basics taught to them. I know this because when I'm teaching leaders, none of them have ever said—*Oh, I learned this ten years ago and you're just reiterating what I already know.* All the way up to VP of HR positions, leaders say they aren't doing what we teach in the program. Why aren't they doing the basics? I don't know. Maybe they're so busy during the workday that they don't feel they have time for the basics. But what kind of baseball players don't do drills?

Taking responsibility for output and results can feel really good; leaders usually just don't know that when we first meet them. In a way, leaders seem haggard by those concepts and are sometimes too busy putting out fires to do that kind of strategic thinking. **When leaders truly believe they are the captain of their own ship, it feels better to set expectations, manage output, and drive results instead of putting up with confusion and missed targets.** Those good feelings reinforce the process while fueling better and better results.

For example, there was a group of supervisors who had worked on their reviews and commented on how much better the process had gone. When I asked why, they let me know that they helped each other write them. A couple of employee reviews were very problematic, so a few supervisors got their heads together and sorted out the issues and strategized on how to write those reviews. Another one became an even bigger problem, so they also wrote that review together. They described how they got better at writing reviews by helping each other. Getting more input was key.

One of them said, "When I described what I didn't like, they helped me put it into words, challenged my thinking, and even showed me what I hadn't seen before."

The supervisors began to realize that getting input helped them communicate more effectively in their review. The added input gave them a larger perspective, and that insight helped them to write a better review. The supervisors respectfully communicated their problematic reviews to HR, filling them in about everything the supervisors had thought and talked about together. **When leaders grow into a coaching style of leadership, they don't need HR to solve problems on their teams as much as they have in the past.**

How to Stop the Churn and Burn

Before learning and reinforcing the good feelings that come with getting the support they need from other leaders, those supervisors would have gone to HR. They wouldn't have known what to do to change their team members' behavior. Also, they probably would have gotten into a lot of blaming, saying things like—*Something's wrong with my people, I don't have good people, They don't care, They're not wired right, They aren't doing it the way I want them to do it, I need to get the right person, This is maybe not a good fit.* It's also likely they would have begun to experience some self-doubt about whether they hired the wrong person. But they haven't begun to develop that person. They haven't even put their big toe in the water of coaching.

When leaders move from blame to clarity, they stop wasting time and churning through people. Team members know they're being blamed because somehow they haven't guessed the right way to do their job. They've never been told or supported. Imagine what employees must be thinking, *I haven't magically been a fit for what you're looking for because you haven't told me.* So many people end up getting fired or leaving jobs simply because the leader was unable to figure out how to be clear. There is a huge price tag for this confusion, which is why we dedicate our program to getting organizations out of this cycle.

Effective Leadership Feels Good

In my experience, by the time leaders bring people before HR, the situation is so badly broken and has probably been out of whack for so long that it's hard to find a fix. The more the leader knows what to do and takes on that responsibility, the easier it becomes to alter this very common, yet damaging, scenario. There are very few lost causes. But there are people who are not willing to do the job, people who can't do the job, or both.

In this softer, gentler society concerned with developing people, organizations frequently ask about these types of people. How do they handle them? My answer is always the same. They may have some people in their population who don't want to be there. **But why would an organization manage one hundred percent of its population according to what three percent needs?** Their goal must be to get clear on who they are as quickly and clearly as possible and take care of it through the right channels and proper documentation. But these situations happen less often when confident leaders take responsibility for their teams.

There's a powerful shift from an environment where stressed leaders are confused and blaming, to one where confident leaders are clear and taking responsibility to get the work done in a positive manner. These reinforcements improve workplaces dramatically when the whole organization is engaged. It's one of the reasons why we always work top to bottom, right to left in CORE. We don't want pockets of coaching. We want a pervasive shift. In order to do this, the program needs to be mandatory. Everybody needs community, practice, and clarity—not just certain groups of people. And when organizations do make this commitment, then the coaching style and its many benefits pervade the culture.

Again, we must ask the question—What is more disrespectful than giving people a job and then setting them up to fail? Supervisors and leaders can't expect their teams to do what they aren't capable of, especially if they haven't been trained or given the support they need. When we point this out to leaders, they readily understand the idea that if they haven't set their people up for success, they've failed as a leader. But until we talk about it at length, they just don't see it.

Many companies seek out the CORE program because they did some form of continuous improvement or operational excellence, but couldn't get those concepts or the improvements to take hold. Lots of times it's because they were implementing the teachings in an artificial way, meaning they tended to treat people like objects. For example, the organization's thought process could go something like—*we're going to put you in this continuous improvement event, you're going to fix this process and make it better.*

In this kind of two-dimensional approach, employees need to cooperate with what the organization tells them to do. However, nothing sustainable works this way. Leadership needs to take the time to support their people when making any type of change in how they think, feel, or work. Leaders can only do that through relationships and showing they care. Reinforcements are surprisingly second nature when the organization has developed its people—all of its people—to buy into the many benefits of a coaching leadership style.

HAPPY LEADERS CREATE HAPPY TEAMS

We discovered an incredible surprise when we witnessed how reinforcement became second nature across hundreds of organizations. In our experience, reinforcing a coaching style of leadership begins with the leaders who are hired, is sustained by how they support those leaders and their teams, and is strengthened by how they choose to recognize their employees.

How does an organization begin to reinforce its employees?

It begins by being aware of its many benefits—engaging team members to want to drive performance; sustaining that engagement through commitment, practice, accountability, the correct habits, and community support; mastering leadership skills to build confidence, reduce stress, and have a more enjoyable workplace; and activating, building, and sustaining respectful relationships in the workplace.

Reinforcement seems like a complicated idea when leaders first think about it. But, as we work with them, we hear the same thing from program participants—they all want the many benefits and are motivated to encourage the kind of reinforcements to make them happen. Leaders won't make this kind of sea change just to improve business. That alone isn't a big enough motivator when there is so much work to do to make the transformation.

Making this second nature sounds amazing, but they don't know where to start. Instead of the thrill of being the only one to solve every problem, leaders pivot to the good feelings that come from supporting and nurturing the talents of their team, so that the team can develop their skills and use their talents to create their own solid solutions. To keep the good vibrations going, leaders need to practice feeling good.

LEADERS NEED DRILLS

Leadership needs practice to effectively set clear expectations, educate teams in block-and-tackle training to teach skills, practice those skills, give important feedback, and seek support. Rinse and Repeat.

How to go about these drills is as simple as it is obvious. Leaders need to spend one to two hours per month in order to stay in connection with each other and keep up a practice schedule. We have to practice practicing so we provide the time and space for communication and role-play to occur. For example, if football players are going to play on Sunday, they do drills Monday through Friday. Similarly, leaders can do the same. The drill could be to ask leaders to pick something that's not happening that they want to accomplish during a particular week. What got in the way? Once they spend some time acknowledging those hurdles, they could use all their skills to practice finding a solution, like getting support.

> **Leaders must consistently practice to
> be consistently good at leadership.**

Like a musician who practices regularly to be good at playing an instrument, leaders need to practice being good leaders. When it comes time to just connect and be real, every leader still has to practice—I don't care how long they've been leading or how many drills they know. This idea gets to the heart of why the long-term approach has been so successful. In year two, leaders teach others in the program. And, as they teach, they learn the material in new ways. As leaders run the drills, they understand them from a new angle. When leaders become teachers, they learn even more than when they were students.

Ineffective leaders are generally just leaders in need of more skills, and/or more care and support. The idea that a company has bad people, or there's something wrong with their people, or that they don't care, is a misperception. There's nothing wrong with their humans. The company simply has unskilled leaders…until those leaders practice.

When leaders start practicing, they are busy being a novice. There's a lot of doubt and questioning and maybe a lack of self-confidence. Then they come through the program a second time, and they say things like—*I'm getting it, it's coming faster.* Then they come through a third time, and they've gained mastery. They know how to think about certain situations and how to get answers to their questions.

How do I know a 24/7 leader? When they arrive at mastery. The first level of learning simply isn't adequate for anyone to lead 24/7, especially for anybody supervising the supervisors. Leaders have to be strong, and that comes through practice. They have to know coaching well enough to teach the program. Otherwise, leaders may face a situation where a supervisor on their team says, "I don't know how to get my results." And the leader, their boss, won't know how either.

WHAT GREAT LEADERSHIP LOOKS LIKE

It is such a joy to see an organization break out of poor leadership, stress, and sniping to move in a more powerful direction. Happiness is contagious (so is backbiting) and changes the entire atmosphere of an organization. Leaders support positive changes born from great communication based on respect.

When participants present their final projects, they'll often move several people in the audience, creating a sense of awe. They usually bring in trifold exhibits, like science fair projects. The team that developed a new attendance policy interviewed employees, gathered their ideas, drafted something responsible, and didn't sound authoritative—rather, like a human writing for other humans. Not that many months earlier, they didn't know how to solve big problems. But they found their solutions by getting the support they needed and practicing their skills. This unleashed each team's talents, and those team members brought their solutions home. It actually surprised me how little they needed me. Just as it will surprise you. One of my next big surprises was the power of reflection to help leaders boost their effectiveness.

USING THE POWER OF REFLECTION TO BE A MORE EFFECTIVE LEADER

How do we create the time-outs necessary for reflection? An hour or two each month to accomplish these support sessions creates a much different workplace. To adequately reflect on behaviors and feelings, we have to slow down. Usually, we don't know how we feel because we're too busy reacting. There's more than one way people can connect, but the most important ingredient of these sessions is safety.

Setting ground rules, like not naming names and keeping the topics discussed inside the room, helps to create the right environment to get support. Over time, we found the importance of pausing for leaders to strengthen their approach. We also found that pausing prior to connecting with other leaders helps people have a better sense of their own thoughts before they seek to share them. **Part of showing up effectively in a leadership community is to be in touch with ourselves and what we think and feel.**

CONTINUALLY PRACTICE SETTING TEAMS UP FOR SUCCESS

When we ask, *What results are you seeing that you want to see?* The response typically is, *Well, I haven't set the expectation.* It's easy to see why they struggle with getting the results they want. The concepts we work with are very basic, yet everyone agrees they all need to get better at them. The success of building community starts with setting expectations—setting people up for success. This means that if I'm going to have a person do a job, I need to set them up to be successful. Then, leaders often have a moment that seems to defy logic—saying that they've missed the most obvious thing in their leadership.

When building community, we need to understand what it means to make these expectations clear. *Did I tell them what I wanted done? What did I make sure that they knew how to do to accomplish this? Have I given them the resources to do it?* The reasons leaders skip this basic step vary, but it generally boils down to busy schedules and being in the flow of their work. **It doesn't matter at what level or how long they've been leading, or in what industry. Consistently, across the board,**

leaders cannot pass this first foundational milestone: setting clear expectations with their team.

The way we practice setting teams up for success is by having leaders name some problems they're having with their teams—*What are they not doing that they want their team to do? What are they doing that they don't want their team to do?* After they write them down, we go through the expectations—*Are they clear? Did the team know what they are? Have leaders confirmed that the team knows what they are?*

If we can't get clear on the expectations, then we don't even go through the rest of the diagnostics such as training, skills, coaching, and feedback. It is necessary to practice setting teams up for success through clear expectations. We practice giving clear expectations through a process of communication where we check in with each other. Everybody learns this way. Not in any one-time training.

We call leaders back to the obvious, yet overlooked.

When first beginning this work, I thought it would just be about assessing the basics of leadership that existed within the company, and then teaching them how to become coaches. However, the basics weren't in place to do that. **Two things struck me as I made this startling discovery—People can't do their best work without clear expectations; and when we put people in jobs where they can't succeed, it is disrespectful.**

Organizations need to give leaders the respect they deserve by helping them get that block-and-tackle training to ensure they're good leaders. They learn the skills in the program, practice them, and have the confidence to use them. They don't go through a one-time training. They commit to going the long distance over a few years to create their heart's desire—engaged workers making significant improvements in the organization.

In a way, it is similar to how football players and baseball players practice drills. Even superstars practice them over their entire lifetime in their sport. For example, no basketball player is ever done practicing free throws. It's the same with practicing expectation-setting with team members. Practice makes perfect. We will never be able to say that we're "done" with practicing how to set our teams up for success.

For example, the other day in a session, we discussed negative social behaviors like sarcasm and gossip. Good ground rules included making sure the person giving support wouldn't be a repository for gossip or talking behind someone's back. If someone came to talk about a person who bugged them, they would be supported in how to handle the situation. **Good leadership means that the person needing support would talk to the person in question.**

Leadership development needs to build judgment and capability, while giving supervisors practice using their judgment in community. They will sit down, talk, and listen to each other. By sharing what's going on, they will make some decisions together. Building a supportive community feels good. And when we feel good, we want to keep those good feelings coming.

BE ON YOUR SIDE

Leaders are up to bat every day. A key component to a successful coaching leadership style means guarding against the feeling of discouragement. Many times, leaders will tell me they think they should learn something faster, or they shouldn't make mistakes. Leaders can judge themselves harshly, sometimes suggesting that when leadership is done "right" it should always feel "good." Some believe that improved leadership is a straight line, which it never is.

The journey to a coaching leadership style is longer and harder than most people imagine, let alone talk about. Leaders can only break out of this flawed idea of perfection when they share their authentic struggles with other leaders. Opening up, as we discovered earlier, allows leaders to learn from their peers and get the powerful support they will need to keep trying again, while gaining an awareness of how they could've done better. When I facilitate this type of discussion among leaders, I often hear their realizations about how they would have listened better or asked more informative questions. Discussion with other leaders frequently brings this kind of awareness, which is an important part of growth and an antidote to discouragement.

Leaders give what they get.

A CEO and owner of a company I work with tended to be very critical before stepping into his coaching leadership style. Often, this attitude came from negative self-talk, which he ended up using on his team. If leaders are harsh on themselves, they will be harsh on others. We quickly learned how to get out of that mindset and into one that is more generous to himself and his team. To get past the discouragement of his team, he first needed to learn how to encourage himself.

LEADERS HAVE TO BE ON THEIR OWN SIDE TO OVERCOME MISSTEPS

For example, when kids are learning to ride a bike, their parents don't harshly criticize them when they lose their balance. If they fall off the bike, parents encourage kids to get back on. Leaders need to do the same when they make a misstep. Before they can coach others, they must first be able to coach themselves to keep at it, try again, and not give up.

Mistakes happen. Leaders need a game plan for when they do. But they incorrectly assume they should be perfect because they don't want to get fired or demoted. That is a common, yet unrealistic, fear-based attitude that needs to be shifted. It's about handling mistakes, but also celebrating little and big wins too.

Many things we learn how to do often involve a period of being bad at it for a while.

I'm often surprised by how ingrained negative self-talk can be. The voices can sound like—*I'm not any good at this, I'm too this or too that, I shouldn't think too much of myself, Don't brag.* When these thoughts plague leadership, team members suffer. For example, at one of my sessions, I asked the room full of leaders to come up with a list of ten things they do well. In other words, what makes them a good leader. Many in the room, around thirty percent, painfully tried to complete the exercise. Why? Because they're wired not to think too much of themselves. Their mindset tells them it's not okay to feel good about themselves. To help them shift their mindset, I mentioned it will be hard to be warm and encouraging with their team if they can't generate that kind of compassion for themselves.

If leaders don't think they're very good at anything, how will they be able to coach team members to feel good about their work?

Helping people appreciate what makes them a good leader means working on important issues of self-esteem and confidence. For instance, getting over the idea that sharing legitimate accomplishments feels like "bragging," thinking good things about themselves instead of always criticizing, and believing in themselves—which brings about a more peaceful, powerful thought process. When the program bolsters leaders' self-esteem and confidence, they are better able to encourage their team members to try again and not give up when things miss the mark.

It's hard to give something away that you cannot do for yourself. Creating a safe environment that allows people to challenge themselves to think differently, make mistakes, and change the process involves a leader who has the same tolerance for themself. This begins by having the awareness of when self-talk is judgmental, critical, and defeatist, so leaders can shift them into positive, helpful thoughts. We teach these leaders how to do recognition programs at work so they break free of the idea that a hard day's work doesn't deserve recognition.

Why would we want to be convinced there's nothing special about anybody?

A continuous improvement workplace requires that as the team harnesses its talents, there's also a willingness to find and change mistakes, instead of hiding them. Many leaders wear masks, hiding their vulnerabilities—the very things that can take their leadership to the next level. It reminds me of a leader who ended up bringing his team to new heights. His organization was a very people-centric work environment, but this leader just hadn't been doing well with his team. He had a military background, was stoic and very sarcastic, which could be cutting. A young female supervisor had a really hard time relating to him. After experiencing what I could only describe as the dark night of the soul, he came to a serious place of self-reflection. The epiphany helped him accept that his leadership wasn't working.

Then he shared with the young supervisor and the rest of his team something like, "You know, I haven't always treated people well. I don't show up in a way that's supportive of other people's feelings. I'm really working on these issues and am determined to do better and create a better place to work here."

A few weeks ago, I had lunch with the young supervisor when I was at the organization for a training. She said, "It's a whole new day now. I just love working with him."

What made all the difference? He admitted to being human, realized where he was fallible, shared his vulnerabilities, owned his behavior and mistakes, and said he would work to make it better. Opening up this kind of dialogue helped the team try again. **He got back on track with his team by admitting he was an imperfect leader who addressed his issues, after the pain of changing those issues was less than carrying on the same old way he had before.**

SUPPORTING YOURSELF MEANS ADMITTING YOUR MISTAKES (AND MOVING ON)

But sometimes, leaders don't admit them. What happens when directive micromanagers are unwilling or unable to be vulnerable? One time, I guided a supervisor on a coaching call who asked this question. I pointed out that if she wanted a person to be vulnerable and transparent, she also needed to be vulnerable and transparent with the leader. **We show up in conversations the way we want people to show up with us.** If we talk about the things we're reflecting on and where we're struggling, that creates a safe environment for the other person to do so too. We literally model how to drop the mask.

I had a meeting with the one-time stoic leader the other day and shared the feedback his young supervisor gave about the "new day" in his department. I also wrote a note to his boss about the positive change and copied the leader. This spread the joy of the win and made his boss feel good too. Then I relayed that story to someone else, and now to you. **So the impact of him taking off his mask inspired many others to do the same.**

There's a reason for the trend toward leaders who can create a harmonious, positive workplace, including coaching skills. Command and control leadership has lots of problems. Some of these leaders have a hard time hearing what people try to tell them and, as a result, aren't very effective. Many get overwhelmed. Rather than coach, they overdo—taking too much on themselves—enabling and rescuing their team members, in the guise of saving their people from what needs to happen instead of delegating.

Back to the leader whose dark night of the soul helped him find his coaching style. The other day he said, "Now that we're coming into the fall, we've come up with the objectives for next year. There are seven of them. I have two, and I gave five away. Finally, I'm learning what I should own. I need other people to own these rocks. I just needed support in getting there."

"That's what it looks like. You just got out from under needless work," I said.

When I walk leaders through this kind of transparency with their team, I guide them through the process of receiving feedback from their team members. Sometimes hearing the impact they've had on others can be painful. But we do everything we can to support them and care for them during the process. And as they hear feedback, they may have that dark-night-of-the-soul moment that causes them to remove their mask.

The reverse can also be true. Perhaps a leader wants a team member to do something, but they say they aren't willing or able to do what is required. The first thing I always suggest is to get rid of all the negative emotions that will arise. Frustration, anger, and judgment will only get in the way of a coaching style of leadership. Negativity clouds thinking, and as we touched on before, will cause leaders to react instead of respond.

Discussions can be had around what moving forward would look like. Perhaps that's leaving to pursue a new opportunity that would be a better fit, or searching for an environment that would work better. Most importantly, the discussion doesn't have to be full of hostility and conflict, but rather care for the team member. Taking the time to acknowledge and move away from negative emotions slows the process down, so it is easier to respond rather than react.

DON'T LET DISCOURAGEMENT SLOW YOU DOWN

I realized that leaders have a hard time "trying again" because someone gave them the responsibility to run a department or be in charge of something, expecting them to automatically accomplish their new roles perfectly. Organizations don't seem to support transitions to leadership, so lots of leaders end up getting overwhelmed and have trouble adapting to their new roles—let alone feeling comfortable enough to share that experience, which is what makes a great leader. For instance, we can work closely together over the years with fellow team members. We get friendly, going out for drinks after work and knowing whose kids are getting married. But we won't typically share our leadership struggles or how we feel about those challenges. Vulnerability isn't a space we inhabit easily.

But, when we tell each other how we really feel, like we aren't having an easy time, or we're having difficulty letting go of our worries—the needle moves on resilience. We begin coaching each other to be better leaders. For example, if a bunch of micromanagers all talked about the struggles of micromanagement, they'd stop micromanaging. They'd begin to share that struggle, where they want to be, and somehow that support would make the difference. I've seen it with my own eyes every day for decades.

Perhaps one leader shares that he tried hard, but still ended up micromanaging. Then the person sitting next to him says she screwed up but got back in, didn't micromanage, and saw how the process worked better. Another talks about how sometimes we make mistakes and go backwards, but we keep moving the dial forward on changing our habits. They talk about the ups and downs, but also realize that it's just about working on leadership one day at a time, getting each interaction to go well. Our first major lesson in the transformation of traditional leadership into a new coaching style involves building community and sharing leadership experiences. The experience of an increased sense of community also supports leaders' understanding of their own fallacies.

Changes occur through a series of conversations and interactions, and can't be built faster than one conversation at a time, one day at a time.

That is why developing a coaching style of leadership is a journey, not a destination, and can't be mastered completely. It takes time to build the skills for new leadership habits—long enough to understand how leaders are wired and for them to change the way they see themselves as leaders. This transformation involves shifting motivations, thoughts, and behaviors to create new, sustainable habits. Organizations need more realistic ideas about the time it takes for people to change. The coaching skills that create more independent team members demand big changes in leaders, internally and externally.

The key to trying again is to battle discouragement.

It's about leaving what didn't work in the past and moving forward with the philosophy that tomorrow is a new day. After all, who wants to pile discouragement on top of discouragement? If we slip up and eat that ice cream cone on a diet, we can't get so discouraged that we don't bother trying again. We stay positive so that the next day we won't get upset when we get it wrong. **Positivity drives an attitude of wanting to try again.**

Creating personal reminders helps to keep those positive ideas top of mind, like how to show up in a meeting, or to ask more questions. To coach a team into solving their own problems, it's important to interrupt old negative patterns. Ways to do this include listening to podcasts or reading books like *The Coaching Habit*. It also comes from support, reminders, and practice. Signs that display words of encouragement in the office are anchors, reminding people during their busy day to pause and reflect, and do all the things they can to stay focused on their coaching style of leadership.

We ask leaders to list some things they have done to build new habits in their lives—be it working out, a change of diet, quitting smoking, etc. They usually give me a laundry list. Then I let them know the same process is at work here. They will use the same techniques they used to change any other behavior and apply them to coaching their team members to be more independent. In the same way, leaders will learn to try and try again.

ENCOURAGEMENT STARTS WITH COMMUNITY AND SHARING

Sometimes you hear people talk about beginning a workout routine, then going to the gym makes them sick or they get off track. At that point, they try to figure out what it would take to get back to working out regularly. Do you try again when a good habit gets interrupted? I've worked in meditation practices where I've gotten sidetracked sometimes. As we've discussed earlier, building the type of leadership skills that lead to independent team members requires the same regular practice. We have found that leaders need opportunities for regular practice sessions, calling them back to the thoughts and ideas that will bring them out of discouragement and setbacks and foster the resilience needed to keep trying to be a coach.

This kind of regular reinforcement is how people change. They don't change because there's been a directive, but in their own way at their own time. The best way to help is by gently reminding people of how to try again, and thereby creating fertile soil for a coaching style of leadership. Everyone needs to make their own decision about how to lead, and there are a lot of small personal decisions that go into creating a style that works. Encouragement is the key. In the second year of the program, leaders teach each other the training. **When leaders teach others how to be better leaders, they will be better leaders.**

The way to test the soil to make sure it's fertile for a coaching style of leadership is to do assessments. When I work in a typical large environment of fifty leaders, many will need help with micromanagement, and abrasive or abusive leadership styles. When left unchecked, organizations mostly react to those problems. Knowing what types of leaders are in an organization involves assessment.

I've created mechanisms to monitor leadership styles—

- Is the leader able to give feedback?
- Are they able to be kind?
- Does the organization check in with the leader's team?
- What mechanisms are used to monitor them?

When organizations ignore bad leadership, it runs rampant. Then, bad management manages the organization. Assessment holds leaders accountable to the organization and themselves. The average working environment lets bad leadership ride, waiting for people to quit or for issues to bubble up until there are bigger problems. That's not a good way to tend to the soil of leadership. In this case, good leaders come by chance.

But, good leaders aren't accidentally grown.

The person who has had the most impact on my leadership is a mentor I've known for twenty years. I've tended to be over-prescriptive, meaning my thinking goes something like—*Oh, this needs to be done? Well, we will do "x," "y," and "z" to get it accomplished.*

And he'd always say, "Get them to do it. Get them to see it, get them to decide that, get them to create that thing."

He always taught me to take a step back. And this typically happens for participants in year one of the program. Like them, I would go back and practice stepping back a few times. After not seeing him for a while, we would get back together to work on something, and he kept showing me again how I needed to *get them to do it*. I only learned this skill because he taught it to me over time, with his kind reminders and encouragement.

GOOD LEADERSHIP IS ABOUT "GETTING THEM TO DO IT"

Leadership isn't about being ahead of people. Leadership is about being behind people and giving them room to act. It's a very different feeling, and I've had to try again many times to fully understand. It's funny, because now when I see my mentor, I automatically think—*Oh, I'm going to have to try again! One more time, from the top!* He always has a gentle way of reminding me to let the team do it. As my mentor did with me, I've also had to remind leaders that they're going ahead of their team too much. I also gently remind them to back up a few steps.

As we've discussed, learning to do anything differently takes time. Resilience is something you have to be dedicated to in the long run. And progress is made in small stages. Many people who have been with me over the last twenty years have felt the influence of my mentor on my leadership. But sometimes I didn't realize I had been making progress because *letting them do it* didn't look like what I thought it would. We sometimes think we have gotten nowhere. But we are progressing. There's no finish line to continual improvement or good leadership.

The lesson my mentor taught me over time, with encouragement, has always been a powerful one for me. You don't just tell a team to do something. Rather, put a ball in the middle of the room and then watch how they approach it and how they play. We allow them to have their own interactions with the ball, instead of controlling them with our own limited perspective.

Let others' unique thinking drive solutions.

PART III

THE WISDOM
OF LEADING BETTER

Why do workplaces have so few in leadership positions holding power over everyone else? Traditional hierarchies look like a pyramid, so there are fewer people at the top. It starts with the c-suite, then further down, the leadership team increases to about ten or twelve, followed by a layer of thirty managers. If an organization has around thirteen hundred people, we end up with ninety or more supervisors. This means that over time, we have accepted that leaders make up only ten percent of the workforce, excluding the rest.

In continuous improvement workplaces, which optimize the talents of each individual, the pyramid opens up and looks more like a goal post. In this way, everyone becomes a leader, except for new hires. However, people don't become leaders over others. Instead, they exercise personal leadership by making improvements, managing processes, and contributing more fully to the extent of their abilities. In a coaching leadership style, we hone leadership skills in each individual. There's no reason to require that such a small percentage of people in a company do what the rest of the adults can do.

Coaching your team members to be more independent is a disruptive idea that is also simple, obvious, and one of the most challenging ventures leadership teams attempt. We've tried to boil it all down to the essential six habits and the ways to build them successfully from years of trial and practice. We've learned a lot about how to create a coaching style of leadership together.

In closing, let's summarize what we've learned and take some inspiration from a dancing guy and a flock of geese—two concepts that have meant a great deal to me during my career.

THE DANCING GUY

In a YouTube video I love, we meet a lone guy dancing at a crowded concert venue where everyone else in the audience sits on the grass. He's a dancing fool, really into it, dancing like there's no tomorrow. He looks crazy until he's joined by his first follower. The dancing guy acknowledges the new follower with fist bumps as they dance around each other. Boy, does it look fun.

The three-minute-ish video shows a movement happening in real time and leaves us with some important leadership lessons. A leader—in this case, the dancing guy—needs to be able to stand out alone and look ridiculous. Since he's easy to follow (has clear expectations), he gains his first follower. As the video points out, it takes guts to be a first follower because they risk ridicule. Then, the new guy calls his friends to join in and shows everyone else how to follow.

The dancing guy embraces everyone who joins him as an equal, so it's not about the leader anymore, it's about the group dancing together.

He goes from being a lone nut to inspiring a crowd that creates buzz. It's important that outsiders see more than just the leader dancing, because followers inspire new followers. As more people jump in, following is no longer risky. If people were on the fence before, there's no reason not to join because they won't stand out or be ridiculed.

"If you are a version of the shirtless dancing guy all alone, remember the importance of nurturing your first few followers as equals. Make everything clearly about the movement, not you. Be public. Be easy to follow. But the biggest lesson here? Did you catch it? Leadership is over glorified. Yes, it started with the shirtless guy, and he'll get all the credit. But you saw what really happened. It was the first follower that transformed a lone nut into a leader. There's no movement without the first follower. See, we're told that we all need to be leaders, but that would be really ineffective. The best way to make a movement, if you really care, is to courageously follow and show others how to follow. When you find a lone nut doing something great, have the guts to be the first person to stand up and join." —*How to Start a Movement: Leadership Lessons from Dancing Guy,* YouTube

When I came across the Dancing Guy video many years ago, it created a distinct shift in my approach to the field of Lean HR. I felt like the lone nut who kept insisting that HR needs to take a strong leadership role in continuous improvement strategies. The video hit me like a ton of bricks. My powerful insight wouldn't gain traction if I didn't encourage my followers to make continuous improvement strategies the focus of other HR leaders. I began asking folks to speak, write, and share their journeys with others. When people asked me how to get their HR teams more involved, I emphatically stated that, in my experience, they would generally only listen to other HR folks. This gave me the idea to work in a way that supports a community of HR people who talk to each other to consider better ways of doing things.

It is just as important for leaders to consider how they inspire followers to lead. As the years have gone on since first watching the Dancing Guy, I continue to consider the need for there to be followers well beyond my lone nut dance. In fact, this general practice of handing the baton to others has led to a realization that the program needs to be taught by the leaders and not trainers. People learn by teaching. Leaders look to their leaders for guidance, so they need to see their leaders teaching the concepts. When a "trainer" taught, I saw a wasted opportunity for the leadership community to practice amongst themselves.

This idea runs counter to current training. When leaders are put in the loop, they have a direct outcome in achieving the results. Teams look to their leaders as their coach, not to just support the training. In fact, the actual specific hours of training are only a drop in the bucket in the process of building coaching skills. It is important to ensure that leaders are available to provide coaching and guidance for the long haul.

Now, it's your turn to get someone to dance.

WISDOM OF THE GEESE

This video always makes me cry, so I usually leave the room when I play it for leaders in the program. It talks about how we don't set out to become leaders, but rather set out to make a difference in the world. In my case, it meant driving my parents crazy, eventually becoming rebellious enough to spend my adult life disrupting the way people lead. This video shows how geese succeed and take care of each other throughout their lives. So often, I've found that good business leadership transcends the walls of our companies and **follows us home,** helping to transform our personal relationships as well.

GOOD BUSINESS LEADERSHIP FOLLOWS US HOME

I often hear people in the program say that they are doing so much better with their kids. They'll talk about the similarities between the performance cycle we learn in the program and how they help their families at home—like setting expectations, making sure people know how to do things, coaching with support, and positive recognition.

One guy pulled me aside the other day and said, "I used what I learned in CORE with my fourteen-year-old, and I also explained to him that as he grew up, these would be the skills that he'll need to be successful in the workplace." I never thought of these concepts as parenting tools, but people find that when they ask more questions like we do in the program, they build better relationships, period.

Want better relationships? Ask more questions.

People in the program have said things like, *I'm asking more questions. I'm realizing when I'm emotionally triggered and how to manage that and then get more curious instead of coming at them.* Because of what we practiced in the workplace, they see what doesn't work well and what does. Then they use that information to help all their relationships, and that builds a stronger sense of community.

Great leadership is about working on a team, just like a flock of geese. Their common goal of migration can only occur when they flap their wings, creating uplift for the whole flock as they ride the currents together, reducing air friction for the birds that follow. Their "V" formation helps them travel farther, faster. Ever since I first saw this video, I put it in practice when considering a variety of organizational meetings. I'm always suggesting to leaders that until you can make sure everybody on your team can run that meeting, you're not using the wisdom of the geese because every person must be able to follow and lead.

Bottom-up and top-down visibility helps everyone see the bigger picture, and get better aligned with the organization's vision. Like geese, a sense of community emerges when people work as a team. They've learned that their teamwork, common direction, and vision get them to their destination quicker with greater ease because they benefit from the momentum of the group.

"If we have as much sense as a goose, we will stay in formation, joining those heading in the direction that we want to go. The sense of community emerges with a willingness to work as a team." —*Wisdom of the Geese*, YouTube

It is second nature for geese to support each other. When the lead goose tires, it rotates to the back of the formation so another goose can take over, moving back in the line-up to allow another goose to take the lead. Tight control of the flock would burn a lead goose out. Nature doesn't micromanage, and neither should we. Micromanagement leads to the burnout and disengagement of teams. People have unique skills and talents to offer, and giving them autonomy and the opportunity to shine will not only showcase those abilities, but build confidence and grow the organization from the inside out, reaching surprising outcomes.

The lessons we can learn about how geese support each other is why I have to leave the room every time I play the video. Their dedication and support for each other just chokes me up. When one goose falls out of formation and suddenly feels strong headwinds, it automatically makes adjustments to draft off the bird in front of it. As leaders, we need the humility to open up and become vulnerable with our team about the challenges we face and to seek help as soon as we get stuck. When we get vulnerable and openly communicate our struggles, our team will move faster and achieve more.

"If we have the sense of a goose, we will openly and confidently acknowledge when we need help and gratefully accept the support that is offered and will fly harder to stay up with the flock so we can all go longer distances with ease."—*Wisdom of the Geese*, YouTube

Have you ever heard the call of the geese as they fly? That is the sound of the flock encouraging each other to keep up their speed. Leaders should always recognize great work. We need to praise people and give them the recognition they deserve. Lack of recognition is one of the main reasons for disengagement, and is all too common in busy, fast-paced work environments. But it's vital to the team and the organization that leaders constantly reinforce great work and encourage others to motivate people to achieve their goals.

But the real tear-jerker happens (and I actually have to leave the room) when a goose gets sick and two other geese drop out of the formation and escort it down for protection. They will stay with that sick bird until it dies or is able to fly again. Then, they either catch up to their flock or join another. I yearn for humans to be that diligent in how they care for each other. Where there's no need to ask for help because we would just help. Any one of us could need help, and someone would just show up. I can't watch this part with a dry eye because I long for their instinctive helping nature to become our second nature.

Why is it that humans haven't learned how to help and receive help?

Leaders need to stand by each other in difficult times. When the going gets tough and people are facing challenges, that's when teams need us the most, through strong personal relationships forged by open communication—not punitive policies that punish. The wisdom of the geese teaches us to stand by each other when things get rough, and willingly take the support and guidance that's offered.

In the end, the video teaches us that geese never vary their migration routes. They use the same flight pattern year after year, even when different geese join and leave the flock. The young learn the route from their parents. The takeaway for us is to remember that things change for an organization to remain agile, but great organizations stick to their core purpose and values.

The geese demonstrate many lessons of a coaching style of leadership—sharing a common goal, giving everyone equal visibility, the humility to be vulnerable and seek help, empowering others to lead, always recognizing great work, and offering support during challenging times.

"If we have the sense of a goose, we will recover and regroup and resume formation with the greater team headed in the direction that we want to go. And we will stick with the plan until we succeed."

Wisdom of the Geese, YouTube

WISDOM OF CORE

When I'm working with leaders, I always wonder if they will see the concepts as too basic. But with each experience, I always find the same to be true—leaders with the skills admit that they still need to get better at them. Ones who don't have the skills are always surprised at how intuitive the coaching style of leadership is, yet confess it's anything but easy to implement. Most participants tell me that it's really great to have everyone on the same page—getting the entire leadership community up to speed with the same level of the same skills and, most importantly, talking the same language.

THE IMPORTANCE OF LONG-TERM APPROACHES

At the end of one of my two-day workshops in the first-year program at an organization we worked with the other day, I said, "I'm so glad I created a one-year program. If not, I'd be standing here now wishing you all good luck with this."

We provide the needed nurturing and support to help leaders in our program learn how to implement their coaching leadership style. After the two-day workshop, organized accountability partners help each other on a week-to-week basis. Then, we come back together in a month to keep practicing. As they practice, they take their learning to the next level.

I've been invested in **long-term approaches** to help organizations successfully implement this coaching leadership style because of the time needed to acquire the habits and the amount of practice it takes for them to become sustainable. Without commitment, the good work of learning the habits dissipates fast. Organizations think the idea of creating a coaching style of leadership and realizing its benefits are great. They might think the foundations are wonderful. But without the commitment to actually make the concepts in this book sustainable, the coaching style just doesn't work.

NARROW YOUR FOCUS TO GET THE HELP YOU NEED

When we do assessments at the beginning and during the program, we learn so many things about what leaders have learned, but also become aware of which concepts they need to practice more. Because all the skills are equally important, they never just work on one thing. Generally, there are several things leaders and their teams need to work on over time. So, the first thing we want to do is make sure people aren't overwhelmed, for example, trying to work on nine different skills at the same time. It's important that people are successful. When they try to do everything, they may end up feeling like they're failing.

What help do you need? You'll want to narrow your focus and know what you're shooting for so you can achieve it and feel successful.

For example, if a leader wants to ask more questions, they learn how to set it up so they can clearly achieve that goal. This might look like, *I asked one more question a day than I did yesterday, I'll try and ask one question a day.* This helps leaders and their teams recognize how to bite off what they can chew and set them up for success, like we hope they will do with each other. Essentially, we model the behavior we hope to instill in them.

One lady said to me the other day, "I just love it because I realize now that I have a plethora of support."

Support shows up in everything we ever do, so no one has to do it alone. Most times, I work with groups of leaders who have never spent so much time together, much less think of each other as a community of support. They are used to thinking in terms of an organization chart. To get that kind of community support, the leaders have made the decision to become vulnerable with each other.

CONNECTING WITH YOUR TEAM HELPS YOU REALIZE YOU ARE NOT ALONE

I always conclude work sessions by asking leaders —*What are you grateful for as you stand here now?* Usually, people say that they are really grateful to their teammates and leaders for being transparent and willing to share and take risks. Not only do I absolutely love witnessing the growth of leadership skills they acquire and encourage in others, but they enjoy watching each other grow.

Leaders realize they're not alone and are just as happy to be the one helping as the one being helped.

Like the geese, they begin to feel really connected with each other and that they are in this together. Until then, I don't think they ever really had that feeling. Sure, they'd be on projects together, but there wasn't a shared common goal and a commitment to see each other through their challenges. Usually, the experience felt lonely and had the effect of disengaging even the most talented workers.

HOW "BALANCING THE LINES" CAN HELP YOU SOLVE PROBLEMS

To counter that, we create the time and place for people to really get vulnerable and share what's happening. If they don't continually practice, then they go back to business as usual. The demands of the job can erase the time and places for people to really connect at that level. Essentially, without the proper support, they end up dismantling the very thing we've worked so hard to create, which is a community.

During these private times, we share, explore, and support each other to solve problems. Instead of being too busy because of that next new product launch, creating business goals, or the pressure of other weighty strategies and tactics, we give people time to get out of the weeds of work and share what's going on, their struggles, and their challenges. This awareness needs the proper time to foster so that it becomes a long-term practice. As humans, our need for this type of practice doesn't dissipate.

In Lean, we call this balancing. In general, when products are being manufactured, they'll occasionally get stopped up somewhere, which can create bottlenecks. They call this "balancing the lines." I always feel like that is what we're doing in CORE: eliminating the bottlenecks.

How did I get good at this? The same way you will. When I leave my team, I have the same issues you do. And I don't get through them any differently than I teach—getting support, revisiting the concepts, practicing the concepts. I haven't found any shortcuts around those simple, important steps.

> **We're balancing leadership skills—letting stronger leaders help the weaker ones until they're more balanced.**

Usually, the weakest leaders are a problem nobody knows how to address. That's a big problem and can cause the kind of stuckness that creates a fair amount of damage to the organization's culture. It can cause people to quit, leave, shift departments, or worse—become unhappy, which tends to color the attitudes of other people on the team. A coaching style of leadership is the only thing that actually handles these kinds of organization-damaging problems. It's one of the reasons I've been so excited and committed to helping leaders become coaches. **If you're trying to coach leaders individually, it's just an uphill battle. They need more help. They need more lift.**

LIFTING EACH OTHER UP BUILDS RELATIONSHIPS

And when we achieve that lift, the results are staggering for the company and beyond. It actually changes lives. At one point in the program, we focus on "care notes"—little handwritten cards that specifically recognize something a teammate has done, what it meant to us, and the impact it had.

During this part of the program, one of the men said, "I went home and wrote a care note to my fiancée because that exercise was so delightful. I've never written a note like that to anybody. The one I wrote to her wasn't just a love note. It was really a way of expressing appreciation for something she'd done for me. You know, it really made a difference in our relationship."

That speaks to how embedded the skills get. The impact of the program is so profound you don't leave them at work. When we begin, workplaces have few leadership positions holding power over everyone else. As we work together, everyone drives the organization, their families, and communities to lead through influence rather than authority.

The power of leadership doesn't come from without, it comes from within.

To foster that kind of power, we always encourage leaders to be on their own side. One of the exercises we do involves making a list of five to ten things they do well as a leader. As we touched on earlier, most leaders struggle with that. But during the process, I point out that before we can support others, we need to be able to support ourselves to grow and learn.

It's really about reminding leaders and their teams to be gentle and encouraging with themselves—to go slow and easy. Because if they come at things hard and convince themselves they're failing and no good, it doesn't help them learn and grow. I encourage them to think of their improvement over the long haul. For example, if they see something they didn't do, instead of berating themselves, it's important to simply realize it was just a missed opportunity, and to acknowledge there will be another opportunity. There are lots of opportunities. That's how to help make sure people don't give up. People need to be good to themselves and encouraging if they're going to be a good coach to others.

Good leadership starts with knowing ourselves.

164

Coaching is a huge shift that takes place within the heart, which is why the work we do with people is so gratifying—I call it soul satisfying. My heart and soul is about creating rich workplaces by building relationships, and I can't wait for you to be able to unleash all that your organization can be when you use these simple, yet profound, concepts.

WAYS TO BECOME A BETTER LEADER

Ready for your organization to implement stronger fundamental leadership skills in order to create the coaches that your organization needs? Work with my team or implement them on your own, with the help of this book and available resources.

Visit leanleadershipcenter.com/corebook to download additional resources to help you bring the CORE Leadership Program principles and behaviors to your workplace. You'll also discover information there about finding out how to get involved with using the CORE materials. You can also find updates on LinkedIn.

Leave a review on Amazon and help other readers discover *Let Go to Lead* or the CORE program.

A FINAL WORD

Early in my career, I used to say that my work is my church, but not in a religious context. The workplace was simply the place where I wanted to show up the way I wanted to show up in the world. At the time, I led five hundred people and completely devoted myself to figuring out how to best support them. I knew this was my purpose. I believe our spiritual nature is the reason why it's so powerful when we connect with others. We see a bit of ourselves in those we build relationships with. When we connect with each other, amazing things happen beyond anything we expect. I've had a lifetime of serving and supporting leaders and I look forward to sharing my knowledge and my encouragement with you in order to meet and exceed your vision.

ACKNOWLEDGMENTS

The CORE program has been made possible through the support of Helen Cashman from the State of Illinois, Meg Brown from Cambridge Air Solutions, and Melissa Smith at McKee Foods. The care and contributions of Mary Pat Knight in the early days gave me the faith to keep going. The genius of Ellie Rose provided a clear path for finding the best way for people to learn these principles. The support of my team, especially Samantha Hartley, has made this project a joy to complete. Last and most of all, the assistance of Laura Elliott in developing this manuscript made it all possible.

RESOURCES

LINKS:

Bar-Eli, Michael. Azar, Ofer H.. Ritov, Ilana. Keidar-Levin, Yael. Schein, Galit. *Action bias among elite soccer goalkeepers: The case of penalty kicks* – https://citeseerx.ist.psu.edu/viewdoc/download?doi=10.1.1.335.9458&rep=rep1&type=pdf

Gino, Francesca. Staats, Bradley. *Why Organizations Don't Learn: Our traditional obsessions—success, taking action, fitting in, and relying on experts—undermine continuous improvement.* – https://hbr.org/2015/11/why-organizations-dont-learn

The Deloitte Global 2022 Gen Z and Millennial Survey – www2.deloitte.com/global/en/pages/about-deloitte/articles/genzmillennialsurvey.html

Self-Determination Theory – https://www.urmc.rochester.edu/community-health/patient-care/self-determination-theory.aspx

How to Start a Movement – https://www.youtube.com/
watch?v=lbaemWIljeQ

Wisdom of the Geese – https://www.youtube.com/
watch?v=y-ezwb-lyw8

BOOKS:

Bungay Stanier, Michael. *The Advice Trap: Be Humble, Stay Curious & Change the Way You Lead Forever.* Page Two, 2020.

Bungay Stanier, Michael. *The Coaching Habit: Say Less, Ask More & Change the Way You Lead Forever.* Page Two, 2016.

Clark, Timothy R. *The 4 Stages of Psychological Safety: Defining the Path to Inclusion and Innovation.* Berrett-Koehler Publishers, 2020.

Clear, James. *Atomic Habits: Tiny Changes, Remarkable Results. An Easy & Proven Way to Build Good Habits & Break Bad Ones.* Avery Publishing Group, 2018.

Duhigg, Charles. *The Power of Habit: Why We Do What We Do in Life and Business.* Random House Trade Paperbacks, 2012.

Hersey, Dr. Paul. *The Situational Leader.* Warner Books, 1986.

Macey, William H., Benjamin Schneider, Karen M. Barbera, and Scott A. Young. *Employee Engagement: Tools for Analysis, Practice, and Competitive Advantage.* Wiley-Blackwell, 2009.

Reynolds, Marcia. *Coach the Person, Not the Problem.* Berrett-Koehler Publishers, 2020.

Rollnick, Stephen and William R. Miller. *Motivational Interviewing: Helping People Change.* The Guilford Press; Third Edition, 2012.

Schein, Edgar H. and Peter A. *Humble Leadership: The Power of Relationships, Openness, and Trust.* Berrett-Koehler Publishers, 2018.

Schroeder, Dean M. and Alan G. Robinson. *The Idea-Driven Organization: Unlocking the Power in Bottom-Up Ideas.* Berrett-Koehler Publishers, 2014.

Stinnett, Kathleen and John H. Zenger. *The Extraordinary Coach: How the Best Leaders Help Others Grow.* McGraw-Hill Education, 2010.

Womack, James P., Daniel T. Jones, and Daniel Roos. *The Machine That Changed the World.* Free Press, 2007.

ABOUT THE AUTHOR

Cheryl Jekiel is on a mission to create a movement. As the inspirational founder of the Lean Leadership Center, Cheryl embodies the values she encourages companies to embrace: focus on people and effectively achieve your goals. By sharing her invaluable expertise on people strategies, lean manufacturing, and lean leadership culture, she has contributed to the operational excellence of countless visionary organizations around the country.

Cheryl has held strategic leadership positions covering operations and human resources, and she has served as a Chief Operating Officer before returning to her love of advancing human resources to enhance workplaces. As the author of *Lean Human Resources: Redesigning HR Processes for a Culture of Continuous Improvement*, Cheryl is dedicated to advancing HR and continuous improvement cultures as a recognized field. Based in Chicagoland, she lives with her beloved husband and two dogs.

www.ingramcontent.com/pod-product-compliance
Lightning Source LLC
Chambersburg PA
CBHW040755220326
41597CB00029BA/4840